Educational Development

EDUCATIONAL DEVELOPMENT

Dr. R.K. Raghuram

CRESCENT
PUBLISHING CORPORATION

[*The responsibility for the facts stated, conclusions reached and plagiarism, if any, in this book is entirely that of the Author. And the Publisher bears no responsibility for them, whatsoever.*]

Educational Development

First Published : 2009

ISBN 978-81-8342-146-1

Published by :

CRESCENT PUBLISHING CORPORATION
4831/24, Prahlad Street,
Ansari Road, Darya Ganj,
New Delhi - 110002
Ph. : 23272541, 23257835
Fax : 91- 011- 23257835
e-mail : campusbooks@hotmail.com

Printed at :
Roshan Offset Printers
Delhi

Preface

Education has always been a matter of immense priority for societies throughout history, who have sought to educate their people for the production of goods and services, respond creatively to the world they live in or fulfil their aesthetic impulses. Recognised today as an important development index for nations, education brings within its purview a whole host of rigmarole which goes beyond mere literacy. This becomes especially true in the case of developing nations, which are still such in the quagmire of illiteracy and poverty, and have to initiate steps to eradicate these issues. In an era where the goals and objectives of education have undergone a sea change, the development of education becomes crucial matter.

This book in the series on education concerns itself with the topic of education development. As the political, social undergo consultant evolutions and changes, it becomes imperative that these changes are reflected in the educational curriculum, is an indispensable component of this process, a field which demands the best minds of developers and administrators. This manual takes a look at what entails effective education development, teaching problems, infrastructure, curriculum development, etc. It also takes into account current trends and practices in the field, fostering an understanding of the issue which is more relevant. In addition, focus has also been concentrated upon incisively analysing and critiquing education development policies.

It is hoped that the insight and erudition of the book serve well for all the readers.

Dr. R.K. Raghuram

Contents

1

Introduction

Organisation and Administration

In any scheme of educational reconstruction which envisages a large scale development of educational institutions of diverse varieties, it is necessary to consider carefully the administrative machinery that should be responsible for the spread of education and for its orderly development.

In India, the present administrative set up is that in all States there is a Directorate of Education working under the direct control of a Minister who has a Secretary to assist him at the Secretariat level and a Director of Education as the executive head of the Department responsible for offering technical advice to the Minister in all educational matters and for carrying out the policy of the Department. In actual practice the Director of Education has to submit his proposals for the reorganisation and expansion of education to the Minister through the Secretary. This has actually meant that such proposals and policies are subjected to criticisms by the subordinate officers of the Secretariat and are often presented in a form which may be quite different from what was originally conceived by the Director. The Secretary himself may not be fully conversant with these problems as he is frequently transferred from one

Department of the Secretariat to another. If education is not to be treated as a mere administrative problem, we feel that the Director of Education should be mainly responsible to advise the Minister and for this purpose we recommend that where the Director himself is not the Secretary of the Department he should have the status of a Joint Secretary and should have direct access to the Minister. It would of course be open to the Minister when he considers it necessary to consult the Secretary particularly in regard to administrative and financial matters.

Need for Co-ordination

We have noticed that in the States as well as at the Centre different Departments and Ministries have responsibility for various aspects of education for the age period of 10 to 17. Thus, while the Department of Education is responsible for most of the activities connected with school education there are other Ministries which have their own organisation for imparting education of particular types. The Ministry of Agriculture, the Ministry of Industry and Commerce, the Ministry of Transport and Communications and Ministry of Labour, both at the Centre and the States, have under their control, schools of different kinds which cater for the needs of this age group. It has often happened that these different Departments are not in touch with one another's activities nor is the Education Department in a position to coordinate them with a view to increasing efficiency and securing economy of effort. It seems, therefore necessary that there should be a coordinating agency and that problems of a similar nature pertaining to more than one Ministry or Department should be discussed by them thoroughly and a concerted programme of education should be formulated. In some cases, the Departments mainly responsible for producing technicians have not utilised their resources adequately for the furtherance of Technical education by starting suitable types of Technical schools.

The Department of Transport and Communications, for instance, maintains a few Secondary schools of the usual type for the children of its employees. In our view the responsibility for training technicians of various grades should be shared by the Central Department of Railways along with other allied departments. This Department has a large number of workshops, and it is intended that in course of time India will become self-sufficient in the production of railway engines and all varieties of rolling stock and other necessary equipment. It is also desirable that there should be an efficient service for repairing, overhauling and the maintenance of all rolling stock and engines.

We are aware that a certain number of apprentices are trained for employment in the railways, and that in some of the central workshops, work connected with the manufacture and repair of engines and rolling stock is being carried on. But if trained personnel of the required standard and in sufficient number is to be available the facilities need to be expanded and improved. Since the railways are the largest employers of technicians of all grades. it should be one of their main functions to maintain or help in the maintenance of technical schools of different grades to trained skilled labour for their work.

Again during the war, the Department of Commerce and Industry in the Central Government was responsible for starting a number of training institutions for technician and many available workshops in the country were utilised for the purpose. Since the conclusion of the war, a few institutes originally started for this purpose have been kept going by the department where training is given in the craft or trade concerned but no provision has been made for general education. In the coordinated programme of Technical education at this level, agriculture has also a large part to play. It seems to us that such departments should pool their resources and adopt a uniform policy in regard to the training of various types of skilled workers needed for the different industries of the country. We may recall here what we have already stated that in all schemes of Technical education there should be room for an adequate amount of general education without which it is not possible to give intelligent training in technical skill. Moreover, the object of all education at this stage whether technical or general is to ensure that all educated youths are also trained for the efficient discharge of their duties as citizens.

Committee of Ministers

In view of all these considerations we recommend that there should be a committee constituted at the Centre as well as in the States consisting of the different Ministers concerned with the various types of education as well as the Minister for Finance. They must meet and discuss how best the resources of the departments could be pooled for the furtherance of the educational programme. The Minister of Education may be the Chairman and the Director of Education, the Secretary of the Committee.

Co-ordinating Committee of Departmental Heads

At the next level, there is need for a coordinating committee consisting of the departmental heads concerned with the various aspects of education. Here we suggest that heads of departments responsible for education, general, technical, agricultural, commercial and other types should meet and discuss the working of the existing machinery and the possibilities of its expansion and improvement. The Director of Education may be the Convener of this Committee and a Deputy Director of Education may act as Secretary. If there is a Deputy or Joint Director of Technical Education, he should be a member of the Committee. This Committee will have to meet several times a year to review the position and to consider methods of improvement and expansion in all relevant fields.

At the outset the Committee should review the whole educational structure and draw up a master plan showing how the necessary integration can be achieved smoothly and expeditiously in the different types of schools established by the State or Centre. The whole object of this planning would be to avoid duplication, to improve and expand the facilities needed for the different educational institutions and to use them more effectively by their coordination or merging, and to lay down a programme under which special types of education may be progressively provided either in separate institutions or in multipurpose schools. Any department of the States or Centre which is interested in developing a particular branch of education should place such proposals before this Committee. It will thus afford an opportunity for getting an over-all picture of the whole field of education and enable the public and the State to know exactly what is being done and what are the plans proposed for the future.

Director of Education

The Director of Education should be assisted in his work by a number of experts, including a Joint Director of Vocational or Technical Education to give expert advice on Technical education. The various Deputy Directors should deal with particular aspects or grades of education and there should be a Deputy Directress of Education, whose chief responsibility should be to, look after the education of girls, and to see to it that adequate facilities are provided for them in the educational system of the State. She should also be responsible for the development of women's education and for advising on their special needs and problems.

Board of Secondary Education

We recommend that there should be a Board of Secondary Education under the chairmanship of the Director of Education to deal with all details of education at the Secondary stage (general and technical). This board should be composed of persons with wide experience and knowledge-of different aspects of Secondary education. We recommend that it should consist of not more than 25 members, ten of whom should be specially conversant with matters pertaining to Vocational or Technical education.

We suggest the following constitution for the Board which can of course be modified to suit special needs of the States concerned:

— The Joint Director of Vocational Education

— The Director of Agriculture

— The Director of Industries

— One Head of a Polytechnic

— Two representatives nominated by Government from the senior teaching staff of Vocational Schools.

— The Deputy Directress of Women's education.

— Four Headmasters of High schools including headmasters of Multipurpose schools, nominated by government.

— Two representatives of Provincial Secondary Teachers' Association, elected by the Executive of the Association.

— Five nominees of the universities of the region, of whom two shall be professors dealing with Technical education.

— Two distinguished educationists co-opted by the other members of the Board.

— Two persons nominated by the Department and a Principal of a Training College nominated by government.

— One of the Deputy Directors as a Member-Secretary.

Functions of the Boards

The Board will be generally responsible for the following matters:

1) To frame conditions for recognition of High schools, Higher Secondary schools and the qualifications of the teaching staff.

2) To appoint committees of experts to advise on the syllabuses etc., for the different courses of study.

3) To frame courses of study on the recommendation of Expert Committees that may be appointed for this purpose.

4) To draw up panels of question Paper Setters, Chief Examiners and Assistant Examiners.

5) To frame rules prescribing the minimum conditions for selection of Examiners, Assistant Examiners, etc., and generally to frame such other rules as may be necessary for its effective functioning.

6) Generally to advice the Director of Education when required on all matters pertaining to Secondary education.

In this connection we wish to point out that in some States, the Boards which have been recently constituted for the purpose are unweildly in number and some of the interests represented on it are not likely to promote efficiency or harmony. We consider that, if Secondary education is to progress on right lines, the Board must be a compact body mainly composed of experts, whose functions will be limited to the formulation of broad policies. The Board is not expected to function as an executive body which is the province of the Director of Education.

With regard to the conduct of examinations, we recommend that a small committee of the Board, consisting of not more than five members, should be appointed, with the Director of Education or a senior member of the Directorate as Convener. This committee will be responsible for framing its scheme and conducting public examinations and for publishing results. The Director will be assisted in this work by a senior officer with the necessary staff to carry out the day-to-day duties and responsibilities in this connection and to attend to all the details concerning the conduct of examinations.

The executive powers needed to implement the recommendations of the Secondary Education Board will be vested in the Chairman of the Board, the Director of Education. This Board shall ordinarily meet at least twice a year, but may meet on other occasions when summoned by the Chairman or on a requisition made by 1/3rd of the members constituting the Board.

It will have its own office and establishment with a whole-time Office Secretary for that purpose.

Board for Teacher Training Institutions

We have referred to the need to establish many new institutions to train teachers in general as well as in

vocational subjects. While the training of graduates will be arranged in University Colleges the training of undergraduates teachers will be carried on in a large number of centres for the supervision and guidance of which we recommend the establishment of a Board that will lay down the conditions necessary for their proper training. It should also be empowered to suggest for the consideration of the universities any improvements that may be needed in the graduate training programme.

Regarding the conditions of this Board, we suggest that the Director of Education will be the Chairman, with the following as members:

(1) The Joint Director of Education (Technical).

(2) Two heads of secondary grade training institutions.

(3) Two headmasters or headmistresses of schools, one of whom will be connected with vocational education.

(4) A principal of a Polytechnic.

(5) Three persons nominated by the government, one of whom at least shall have experience of vocational education.

(6) A dean of the faculty of teaching and another representative of the faculty nominated by the Vice-Chancellor or Vice-Chancellors of the universities in the State.

The functions of this Board would generally be as follows:

(1) To frame schemes and syllabuses for. the training of undergraduate teachers.

(2) To draw up the condition for recognition of such Secondary grade training centres.

(3) To draw up schemes of examinations for these teachers.

(4) To draw up qualifications necessary for the teachers of the different subjects in the training institutions.

(5) To appoint expert committees wherever necessary and to advise the Board on the schemes of special training necessary in the different vocational subjects of study.

(6) Generally to advise the Director of Education when required on all matters pertaining to teacher training.

Central Advisory Board of Education

The Central Advisory Board of Education constituted by the Central Government has been functioning for many years in order to, advise the Central Government and incidentally the States on all matters pertaining to education at different levels. Composed as it is of representatives of all educational interests as well as States, its deliberations have been very useful and its reports have furnished valuable material both for the States and the Centre. We are of opinion that such a body should continue to function as a coordinating agency to consider all India problems concerning education.

Provincial Advisory Boards

We recommend that provincial Advisory Boards should be constituted in all States to advise the Department in all matters pertaining to education. The Board may function on lines similar to the Central Advisory Board of Education and should be composed of representatives of the teaching profession, the universities, Managements of High schools and Higher Secondary schools, heads of departments dealing with different spheres of education, representatives of Industry, Trade and Commerce, and the Legislature and the general public. The Minister of Education should be the Chairman of the Board and the Director of Education or the Education Secretary should

be the Secretary. This body will advise the Department of Education on all matters pertaining to education, particularly its improvement both in the quality and quantity.

Supervision and Inspection of Schools

Existing Defects

The present system of inspection of schools was subjected to criticism by several witnesses. It Was pointed out that inspections were perfunctory, that the time spent by the Inspector at any particular place was insufficient, that the greater part of this time was taken up with routine work like checking accounts and looking into the administrative aspects of the school. There was not enough time devoted to the academic side and contacts between the Inspectors and teachers were casual. It was also stated that the number of schools entrusted to the care of an Inspector was too large and the range too wide for him to be able to acquaint himself with their work and appreciate their problems; nor was he in a position to advise and guide the teaching staff in improving the work of the school. It occasionally happened that the Inspector instead of being "the friend, philosopher and guide" of the school, behaved in such a critical and unsympathetic way that his visit was looked upon with some degree of apprehension if not of resentment. In our view the true role of an Inspector-for whom we would prefer the term Educational Adviser-is to study the problems of each school, to take a comprehensive view of all its functions and to help the teachers to carry out his advice and recommendations. We also recommend that for special subjects like Physical Education, Domestic Science, Art, Music, etc., there should be attached to the Director's Office certain experts in these subjects who will inspect the different schools periodically and help in improving the standards of teaching.

Selection of Inspectorate

At present the Inspectorate Is made up in diverse ways by different States. In some cases Inspectors are recruited directly to inspectional. posts and while certain academic qualifications are prescribed, experience and other relevant qualifications are not duly emphasised. Once a, person has been chosen for the Inspectorate he often continues in that line till the age of retirement. We are of the view that. a person, to be chosen as an Inspector, should Possess high academic qualifications and should have had teaching. experience in schools for at least ten years, or should have been Headmaster of a High school for a minimum period of three years. In addition to direct recruitment the Inspectors should also be drawn from:

(i) Teachers of ten years' experience.

(ii) Experienced Headmasters of High schools, and

(iii) Qualified staff of Training colleges.

We recommend further that suitable persons from any of these categories may be appointed as Inspectors for a period of three to five years after which they may revert to their original posts. In the initial stages, we suggest that fifty per cent of such posts may be reserved for recruitment on this basis. It is necesary that Professors of Training colleges should be conversant with the work done in the schools; and that Headmasters should likewise have a chance to serve as Inspecting Officers for short periods. This will enable them to appreciate the position of the Inspector and to approach the problems of the schools with greater appreciation of the realities from their own experience.

Duties of Inspectors

The duties of an Inspector are divisible into administrative and academic. The administrative duties relate to the annual inspection of records, accounts, office routine, etc. For this purpose he must have the assistance of a competent staff. With the increase in the number and types of schools, this duty will require a considerable amount of his time it he is to discharge these functions properly and efficiently.

The time needed for the. purpose has necessarily restricted the scope of his activities on the academic side. Moreover, the multiplicity of the subjects taught in the school by specially qualified Staff now makes it very difficult for any single officer, however qualified to inspect them thoroughly and to advise on all their problems. We, therefore, recommend that the academic work of the school should be thoroughly inspected by, a panel of experts with the Inspector as Chairman and this should be done once in three years. We recommend that three persons may be chosen from senior teachers of headmasters to visit schools in the comPany of the Inspector and to spend two or three days with the staff, discussing with them all aspects of-school life-the library and laboratory facilities, the curriculum, the organisation of extra-curricular activities, the use of the holidays and all other problems connected with school activities. Through these full and frank discussions, the inspectors will be in a far better Position to help in the improvement of the school. What is suggested is nothing new-colleges affiliated to universities are visited by, commission of "Parts who inspect their working, discuss their problem and report to the university.

Management and Conditions of Recognition

Types of Managements

During our tour we realised that there were several types of school managements. Among these may be mentioned:

(1) *Schools Managed by the States or the Centre:* These schools are comparatively few in number in the different States. They were at one time intended to be model schools whose general methods of work and organisation might be adopted by those who wished to start schools. We cannot say that at present many of the State schools serve as models. In many respects, in view of the great demand for admission to schools, great laxity in the conditions which were observed previously was noted.

(2) *Other Types of Managements:* The large increase in the number of students anxious to join schools has led to a rapid increase in the number of schools and these have been started by a variety of managements, many of whom were not conversant with the needs of the schools or the methods of their management. There are various types of schools managed by:

   (a) Local bodies such as District Boards or Municipalities;

   (b) Religious organisations and other denominational bodies;

   (c) Registered Trust Boards;

   (d) Certain private bodies;

   (e) Individuals;

Schools Maintained by Local Boards

There are many schools which are maintained by local bodies and though we do not wish to make any unfair generalisation about their efficiency, we have had enough evidence to show that there is considerable need for a, toningup of these institutions.

As in the case of private managements, the Local Boards should have a small executive body for the management of schools. This executive body should not exceed nine members with either District Educational Officer or some nominee of the Directorate as an ex-officio member of the Board. In the case of Municipalities or Panchayats, which have only one school in their charge, the headmaster should be ex-officio member of the Executive Committee. We feel strongly that the board should not interfere with the internal management of the schools concerned, or with the powers and duties of the headmasters.

We regret to note that, in many cases, members of local bodies have not hesitated to assume a responsibility to visit schools, to examine the records and sometimes actually to interfere with the teaching. We think this tendency on the part of individual members of the Local Boards to act as an inspecting agency should be strongly discouraged, and no member should have the right to inspect the school or to call for any statement or documents or in any other way to interfere with its internal management. The President of the Committee alone may be authorised to call for returns or information from. the headmaster.

Defects or complaints should be brought to the notice of the District Educational Officer who may be asked to report on them. It is important to safeguard the status of the headmaster and the teachers, if they are to function efficiently and exert their influence for good over the pupils. This does not obviously, imply that any serious lapse on the part of the teachers should be condoned. What we suggest is that the proper channel for enquiry into all such complaints should be the Headmaster and the District Educational Officer and not the members of the Boards, either collectively or individually.

Religious organisations

A number of religious organisations also conduct schools

in the different States. These organisations have contributed to the expansion of educational facilities and many of them have, on the whole maintained a reasonable level of efficiency in their schools. Some of them, however, suffer from the various defects pointed out elsewhere such as over-crowding and ill-qualified staff. In some cases the recruitment of staff is influenced by religious or sectarian considerations. These trends are also noticeable in schools run by other educational associations. Institutions run by communal organisations are also spread over different parts of the country and some of them are run on lines which have tended to promote unhealthy trends. The manner in which the teachers are selected and in some cases the spirit in which the school is administered are not calculated to promote a broad and healthy national outlook.

Registered trust boards

There are certain registered Trust Boards maintaining schools. It is laid down in some instances, under the terms of the trust deed that the schools should be run exclusively for certain purposes or for certain sections of the population exclusively. This is contrary to the growing trend of opinion that all educational institutions should be open to children of every religion and community. The managements, however, are prepared to open their schools to all, but they are prevented from doing so by the terms of the trust. We recommend that legislation should be passed in such cases to permit the admission of all children to such schools but till that is done they should be eligible to receive grant-in-aid like other schools.

Private managements

A large number of private bodies are at present managing schools. We are of opinion that all such bodies should be registered and should function as registered associations.

Individual managements

There is also a fairly large number of schools which are run as "proprietory schools" by individuals. We feel that no Secondary schools should be run on such lines but that they should be governed by a suitable managing board registered under the Companies Act.

Control over the Opening of Schools

In recent years, the great increase in the number of schools has led to a great laxity in the conditions laid down for starting new schools. Our attention has been drawn to a large number of 'unrecognised schools' in some States and schools run by private individuals without prior consultation or approval of the education authorities concerned. This laxity has unfortunately led to a state of affairs where schools are run more like commercial enterprises than as educational institutions. We have also been given to understand that, in many cases, private individuals or groups of individuals start schools without. proper buildings or equipment and having enrolled a number of students, create a situation where the department has no alternative but to recognise them for the sake of the students, though normally such schools should never have been allowed tc function. Such educational institutions often spring up largely because of the paucity of recognised schools to cater for the needs of an ever-increasing school-going population.

From what has been stated above, it will be obvious that if schools are to be run on proper lines, if educational interests are to be duly stressed and a healthy spirit of citizenship is to be inculcated in the pupils, care should be taken that recognition is given only on clearly defined conditions which will ensure their proper running and the maintenance of the right atmosphere in them.

In certain States representations were made by teachers of privately managed institutions requesting that all schools should be taken over by the State. We are not ourselves in agreement with this view and cannot, therefore, recommend such a course of action. On, the other. hand, we feel that private managements have got an important part, to play in the scheme of education and that if a number of managements conduct schools in a. spirit of emulation calculated to secure greater efficiency and co-ordination they will be better served. If such schools are run side by side with State schools, in an atmosphere of healthy competition, improvements in teaching and other aspects of education will be fostered.

We have drawn attention to the many defects noticed in schools run by private managements but we recognise that some of them have been doing their work very efficiently and should be given every encouragement. It is equally imperative, however, that managements which have failed to reach reasonable level of efficiency or have shown gross irregularities or indifference to educational interest should be given a clear directive to remedy these defects within a definite period.

Attention of the State Governments may be invited to the British Education Act of 1944 which empowers the Ministry of Education to take over such schools which fail to conform to conditions prescribed and run them as State schools for a time, and eventually hand them back to the management concerned if it is found to be in a posit-ion to take over charge. We recommend that, wherever possible, the States should similarly take over such schools. If this is not possible, it should not hesitate to close down such schools and make alternative arrangements for the education of the pupils of those institutions.

Conditions for Recognition of Schools

In many States there are, definite conditions regulating the procedure to be adopted for recognition of schools. We believe that managements are complying with these conditions in such States. We, however, feel it necessary to suggest certain general standards and conditions of recognition which may be adopted with suitable modifications by all States for the purpose.

(1) Individual or proprietory managements should be definitely discouraged. All the managing bodies should be registered and should consist of a limited number of persons. We recommend that the membership of such managing bodies should not exceed fifteen.

In all such managing bodies, the headmaster should be an ex-Officio member. In the case of schools which are to be started in future as well as in case of schools where managements have not already complied with the conditions of recognition, we recommend that a nominee of the Director of Education should be made a member of the managing body. His functions would largely be advisory, and we hope that his presence will help the managing body to understand the conditions to be satisfied for recognition and the measures to be taken for improving its efficiency and its activities. We understand that this procedure has been adopted in the case of colleges affiliated to certain universities and it has been found to work satisfactorily.

(2) No member of the Managing Board should directly or indirectly interfere in the internal administration of the school, the discipline of the students or the duties of teachers.

(3) Where a large educational society is responsible for the starting of the school, the actual management should be delegated to a small board functioning on the lines stated above.

(4) The managing body should be responsible for the passing of the budget for proposals to start new branches of study for correspondence with the Directorate of Education in all matters pertaining to the managements of the school and for the appointment of the teaching staff under definite conditions of service. Every management should draw up definite rules of service wherein the conditions of salary, leave etc., are definitely laid down and every teacher on his appointment should receive a copy of these conditions and execute an agreement for service in the school.

(5) Every management should be required to provide an endowment for the proper running of the school, the amount of the endowment being determined with reference to the number of diversified courses that the school may undertake and the general requirements of efficiency. The finances of the school should be kept separate from those of any other institutions under the same management and the interest or income accruing from the endowment should be shown in the receipts for the year. Full and proper accounts should be maintained, and the acquittance roll should clearly show each teacher's scale of pay and the amount drawn each month by him. Separate accounts should be kept for any special fees levied by the school. These accounts may be kept by the headmaster and scrutinised by an Accountant or Auditor of the school. These accounts should be prepared annually and should be subject to audit by the Department of Education. In regard to special endowments, gifts, etc. made to the school,

a separate register of accounts should be maintained which should also be duly audited, the income accruing therefrom being added to the general endowment fund of the schools.

(6) Every management should satisfy the Directorate of Education that adequate accommodation is available for the running of the school in a satisfactory manner. There should be adequate playgrounds and where possible rest rooms and cafeteria or tiffin rooms where the pupils may have their mid-day meals.

Where the school admits girl students, whether in mixed schools or co-educational institutions separate provisions should be made for retiring rooms and common rooms. We have already recommended that a certain number of women should be on the staff of such schools, and provision should be made as far as possible for their accommodation near the school premises.

(7) The management should satisfy the Directorate of Education that qualified staff is available and will be appointed in accordance with the rules laid down by the Department for affiliations. The conditions of service should be uniform for the whole State, and there should be no difference between teachers in State schools and those in privately managed schools so far as the minimum scale of salary, conditions, security of service and the minimum amenities recommended are concerned.

(8) The number of pupils admitted per class and the total number that should be admitted for the whole school should conform to the instructions of the department, taking into consideration the material facilities and the staff available, as well as the number of subjects for which the school seeks

affiliation. We have already stated that ordinarily we consider 500 as the optimum, 750 as the maximum, except in the case of schools with diversified courses of instruction where the maximum may go up to 1,000 provided that not more than 40 pupils are admitted in any section.

We have noticed that at present there is no limit to the number of divisions that can be opened in each class. Some managements have opened a very large number of sections in their congested premises, thus increasing greatly the total number of students as well as the number of sections which each teacher has to teach. We do not think that this kind of education can possibly be efficient. We, therefore, recommend that the number of sections in each class should be limited, and before any increase in the number of sections is made, the prior approval of the Department of Education should be obtained.

The Department of Education should take note of all factors and limit the number of sections in such a manner that teaching does not reduce itself to a mere mechanical process of repeating the same lesson over and over again in the course of a week.

(9) There is a wide divergence in the scale of fees charged by different managements. While we realise that no uniform scale of fees can be fixed for all institutions, we feel that the scales of fees fixed by managements should be subject to approval by the Department of Education. We recognise that in some schools in view of the amenities provided and the appointment of better trained staff, it is necessary to charge a higher rate of fees. At the same time, we are anxious that the managements should not indiscriminately raise the scale of fees. They should in any case be able to satisfy the department that the

higher fees charged are being actually utilised in the interests of the pupils. At the other extreme, cases have been brought to our notice where neighbouring schools have been entered into unfair competition by lowering the scale of fees and by offering concessions and scholarships merely to attract students. We recommend that in the interest of general efficiency of schools, rules should be framed preventing such undue competition amongst neighbouring schools.

We have noted that a large number of "other fees" are levied by school managements for various purposes, and that the total amount of such fees, in some cases, comes to nearly half the tuition fee charged. We consider that this is too heavy a burden on many pupils which can certainly be lessened by carefully defining the activities for which such additional fee can be levied. It is desirable that some sort of uniform practice should be followed in this matter in each State. We suggest that the question should be looked into by a committee appointed by the Education Department. It should not be open to any management to add arbitrarily to the special fees charged for such activities. It should also be ensured that such fees are spent for the objects for which they are collected. In this connection we have been informed that in one of the States it has been laid down that such fees should be charged once in the year and should not exceed the amount of the tuition fee for a month and the items for which they are to be expended are also specified.

In some institutions, subscriptions or donations are asked for the building fund, sinking fund, etc. on a supposedly voluntary basis. This may lead to abuse and should be discouraged.

(10) We have referred to the fact that a large number of schools is managed by certain denominational agencies or by certain sections or communities. In some of these institutions it has been noticed that recruitment of the teaching staff is confined to the particular caste, creed or section concerned.

In our opinion this is not a desirable practice. Whatever may be the composition of the Managing Board, we are definitely of the opinion that, so far as the school teaching staff Is concerned, it is the duty of the management to gee that no such restrictions are imposed on their selection in the large Interests of the school.

In view of the importance and urgency of providing for diversified courses of instruction, we strongly recommend that in the existing as well as the new schools when diversified courses of study are to be started, liberal financial aid and encouragement should be given. We realise that this would Involve a considerably additional financial burden and we feel that this responsibility may well be shared by the State and Central governments. In all such cases particularly when Technical and Agricultural courses are started, we recommend that the State and Central governments should contribute towards necessary equipment. It would then be the responsibility of the managements to carry on their work, with such grant as the State may be able to give towards meeting their deficit. If this recommendation is not implemented there will be little chance of diversified courses being introduced in the near future.

We have described the conditions which should be fulfilled by educational institutions and reiterate that managements should be required to obtain prior approval of the Director of Education before opening a school which should not be given unless the minimum condition prescribed have been fulfilled. It is advisable that a survey be made in each State of the existing educational facilities and a definite plan be formulated for the opening and location of new schools to meet the growing needs of population.

School Building and Equiptment

Open-Air-Schools

There has been some criticism regarding the construction of school buildings and the type of designs approved for this purpose. Examples have been quoted of schools in open spaces under the shade of trees, with very few permanent buildings constructed for the school. It has been suggested that in a country like India open-air school should be encouraged and the heavy cost of construction of school buildings avoided, at least for the present. We visited some of these open-air schools and we felt that under certain conditions some of the activities of the school may be carried on in the open air during part of the year.

Open-air schools serve a different purpose in other countries. Such schools, under the prevalent climatic conditions cannot possibly be a substitute for properly constructed buildings, but in the cases of certain types of handicapped children open-air schools are necessary and are encouraged. For children affected with tuberculosis and other diseases which require plenty of fresh air, open-air schools are encouraged. In such schools however, admission is limited to children suffering from the particular disease.

Two factors may, however, be noted : (1) The open-Air system lends itself to small groups of students being taught there, and it also requires good shade and a large area for carrying on instruction satisfactorily; (2) while much theoretical instruction in certain subjects may be given in open-air classes it is impossible to certain other subjects unless suitable accommodation is provided for them. Thus the laboratories, libraries and work-shops should be located in buildings suitably constructed. In any case the school requires considerable grounds for the physical education programme to be carried out, for group games and certain of the extra-curricular activities of the school. We have also referred to the need for agricultural farms in schools where agriculture is taught as a practical subject.. Such farms may belong to the school or they may be taken on lease from neighbouring farmers who may rent them for a consideration.

Whatever be the type of school building that is ultimately approved certain important requirements should be fulfilled: (i) sites for buildings and playgrounds; (ii) extent of site required; (iii) type design of school buildings; (iv) easy means of transport or easy accessibility.

Sites for -Buildings and Playgrounds

Selection of a site will depend on whether the school is to be situated in a rural or urban area.

Rural Schools: These schools should be established in villages with a fair amount of population and easily accessible to the surrounding villages. There should also be enough open ground available for playgrounds and extracurricular activities of the school. If a residential school is thought of in the rural area, care must be taken to see that sufficient ground is available for the residence of staff and pupils for out-door games. We have referred to the fact that the school should be a centre for the intellectual, social and physical activities of the community of the neighbourhood, and therefore, it is desirable to see that easy accessibility is secured and that the open area available is also adequate.

Urban Schools: Here a site for a school may present many difficulties. We believe that by encouraging rural schools, the pressure on urban schools will diminish more particularly if residential rural schools are encouraged by the State. The site for an urban school should not be in very congested area or in industrial areas. As far as possible the school should be so located that while facilities for transport of students are available, the school itself should be in an area free from the noise and bustle of city life. Many schools nowadays make their own transport arrangements for the students and this should be encouraged. As in the railways the public transport should be made available to school-going children at a concession rate. In big cities the possibility of locating some of the schools In one area with sufficient playground and open space should be explored with the necessary arrangements for transport.

Playgrounds

Playgrounds and open spaces for students' recreation are essential. It may not always be easy to secure enough playground and open spaces in a crowded city, but such open spaces as are available must be conserved to be utilised by groups of schools, if necessary. It is desirable that in all cities more particularly in the big cities, a Committee representative of the school managements, headmasters, city authorities and others interested in the physical-welfare of the students together with representatives of the State should be organised to promote "Play-centre Movement" and from time to time to see that the playgrounds available in the city are effectively used by the schoolgoing population.

Legislation Acquiring Open Spaces

In this connection we wish to stress the importance of keeping playgrounds and open spaces in the big cities free from encroachments either for industrial purposes or for business concerns or for building programmes. We regret to note that in several cities it has become a regular feature for building programmes to encroach upon these spaces not realising the necessity of keeping such open spaces free and of utilising them for the health and welfare of the youth of the country. In this connection, attention is invited to the Open Spaces Act of 1906 as amended in 1912 to cover open spaces and recreation grounds enacted in the United Kingdom. Under this Act, any park. open space or playing field cannot be encroached upon by any of the local authorities without the matter being placed before the Parliament and a specific sanction being obtained. Consequent upon this wise measure, we find that the open spaces in the large cities in England are still kept as open spaces and in spite of a very heavy building programme, none of these open spaces has been encroached upon. We recommend therefore that the State and Central governments should immediately take steps to see that a survey of open spaces, parks and playing fields in all cities, municipalities and in the bigger villages is made and that a complete record of this is maintained and necessary legislation passed to prevent such encroachment for industrial and commercial purposes or for housing societies without proper sanction by the government. If the youth of the country are to be properly encouraged in physical education and their health improved, we believe, that this is one of the urgent steps that should be taken and we therefore recommend early legislation towards this end.

Where there are open spaces belonging to the State or the Centre in any part of the country, rural or urban, the first consideration that should be borne in mind when any scheme is entertained for the utilisation of such sites is the need for preserving them as open spaces, parks or playgrounds for the community as lungs for the city or the rural area concerned. It is only when these conditions are fully satisfied that the assignment of such open spaces as are under the control of the government for other purposes should be considered. We feel that unless a legislative measure of the kind stated above is passed urgently, open spaces now available for use as play-fields and recreational grounds for the children and the youth of the country would soon be denied to them. We recommend also that wherever such open spaces are available steps should be taken by the State in consultation with the local authorities or the rural community to convert them into suitable playing fields and place them at the disposal of the schools and of the public of the area concerned.

Type and Design of Schools

There are at present rules and regulations prescribing the conditions under which schools be constructed. Provision is made in such schools to see that there is a free circulation of air, proper light, shelter from monsoonish weather, and it is also laid down that the rooms constructed should have a certain minimum area to accommodate a certain number of school children in a class. Attention in this connection is invited to the Report of the School Buildings Committee appointed by the Central Advisory Board of Education in 1941. The Report which is comprehensive has made valuable suggestions regarding the school buildings and their equipment. We believe that every classroom should provide for an area of not less than 10 sq. ft. per student.

We are also of opinion that the number of students in any class. should be limited so that classrooms are constructed to accommodate this number. In some States the number is limited to 30, in others. to 40, but we have noted with regret that in recent years, these numbers have been exceeded; in some cases 50 to 60 pupils are admitted into a class. We feel strongly that at this age period, with a) view to establishing personal contact between the teacher and the taught and to exert a wholsome influence on the pupil, the optimum number that should be admitted to any class should be 30 and the maximum should not exceed 40.

We recommend that in future, schools should be so constructed that they can develop later into the pattern of multipurpose schools affording facilities for more than one type of diversified courses. It is very likely that in the majority of schools owing to limitations of finance and personnel, more than one or other of the diversified forms of instruction may not be possible. But ultimately it is our hope that many schools may be able to afford facilities. for two or more diversified courses. Any type design must therefore take note of this possibility of expansion as well as of the variety of courses that may be provided. We feel for instance that it should be necessary to provide for workshops, for certain laboratories, certain special rooms for drawing, painting or music; etc., and it is desirable that any design for a school building should take these into consideration and so adjust the design that in course, of time without much change of the original building, such additional accommodation may be provided. Even if diversified courses are not provided, it is absolutely necessary to maintain at least a small workshop with the necessary equipment.

We are of opinion that the present trend in certain schools to multiply the number of sections in each class and to increase the total strength in the school should not be encouraged. We regret to say that we, have come across schools where the total number of pupils has exceeded 2,000, each class being divided into 8 to 10 sections. This excessive number has led to a groat deal of laxity not only in the teaching, observation and recording of the work of the individual student, but in the maintenance of discipline and in the relationship that should exist between the teacher and the taught, In certain cases pressure has been brought to bear on the headmasters of schools by managements, by parents' associations and by public bodies and sometimes by the authorities concerned, to admit a much large number of students and even to adopt the double shift system to increase the number of school-going population. The schools under such circumstances have to work like factories and the bad effect upon the education imparted to children of such schools can hardly be exaggerated.

Construction of Schools

The schools must provide for (1) certain amenities for the students such as common room, sanitary conveniences, provision for mid-day meals and refreshments to be taken, and in the case of girl students retiring rooms with necessary conveniences separately; (2) accommodation for teachers with a common room available for them; (3) a reading room and a library; (4) a visitors' room where parent or relations who wish to interview the headmaster may wait; (5) a room for the Headmaster and an office room and a room for the Assistant Headmaster, should such a person be appointed; (6) laboratories and workshops where necessary, such laboratories and workshops being constructed on an approved plan and for a definite number of students.

With reference to the library and the reading room, we have stated elsewhere that the school must be a centre of the intellectual activity of the whole, community particularly in rural areas, and for this purpose, the library and reading room should be so constructed that, out of the school hours, it way be possible for the general public also to use the library under certain prescribed conditions. This is one of the ways in which a school can "go to the community" and educate as well as interest the community in its welfare. We also recommend that wherever and Whenever it is possible, without interfering with the regular programme of school work, the, school premises may be placed at the disposal of the public of the place for any of the general purposes for which there is necessity.

The idea prevalent hitherto that a school building should be utilised only for school purposes should no longer be entertained in view of the larger role the school should play into the general interests of the local community. This will secure a better appreciation of the role of the, school and a better education of the school going population themselves in methods of social Service and in various spheres of activity calculated to benefit the community around. We feel that the more the school benefits the community at large, the more the community itself will assist the school, and many healthy activities can be conducted with the full co-operation of the public of the locality. It should. however, be, clearly understood that the Headmaster is the final authority to decide what activities way be, allowed in the school premises.

There is one other aspect of the design of the school that we have to refer to, in some parts of the country, owing to climate conditions, it will be necessary to have indoor accommodation for physical education. The boys could then take active part in physical exercises in open halls where facilities for recreation can be provided.

Research in Building

One other point which we wish to stress is that both in the type design of schools as well as in the type design of furniture, etc. there is considerable scope for research to make, them suit Indian conditions. This research has not so far been undertaken and we think it could be carried out at the Central Building Research Institute with the joint efforts of the teacher and the architect or engineer concerned. The furniture should suit the age group, height, etc. so as to develop proper sitting postures, etc.

Equipment

The equipment of a school is a matter which requires great care. We regret to say that we have noticed many schools where there was hardly equipment, and subjects were taught under conditions where boys were forced to memorise rather than understand what was taught. In some of the schools we visited, it was quite clear that the laboratories were hardly ever used, except as store houses for odds and ends; theoretical instruction in such important subjects as Physics and Chemistry was given in the classroom. It is obvious that to teach Geography without a proper supply of maps, Elementary Physics without models and instruments, Elementary Chemistry without the rudiments of a laboratory would be giving a theoretical instruction without utilising the many valuable aids, but this is what is exactly happening in certain schools.

We understand that in some universities, definite rules have been framed in this behalf and list of essential equipment needed for each subject and for a certain number of students to be taught in such subjects have been drawn up. It is a condition of affiliation that the minimum equipment as set down should be made available before affiliation can be granted to the college. We recommend that in the case of school also for every subject which requires practical instruction in one form or another and for such subjects where audio-visual aids are essential, directions should be given with regard to the equipment that ought to be made available and the exercises that ought to be provided so as to make the teaching of the subject more instructive and useful to the pupils concerned. We feel this would be all the more necessary. In the diversified courses of study which we are recommending, and unless such a scheme is adopted we are afraid that school may get affiliated for such diversified courses of instructions. without having the necessary equipment and appliances and the theoretical type of instruction will seriously impair the value of such courses. We recommend, therefore, that expert committees should be appointed to lay down the equipment required for each of these diversified courses, including the workshop equipment and the number of pupils that can be conveniently accommodated in the workshop.

Audio-Visual Aids

There are some modern methods of Audio-Visual education used at present in different countries which have yet to be more fully utilised in our schools, and we feel that suitable provision must be made for this purpose. Among such equipment may be mentioned film and filmstrip projectors, radios, magic lanterns and Epidioscopes etc. Such appliances may be shared by two or three schools to be used by them in rotation at different times of the day or on different days. We have referred elsewhere to the part that the radio can play in giving general education to the students of schools and colleges and the close liaison that should be maintained between the teaching staff of the school and those connected with All India Radio. We were very glad to know that in many States such a close liaison is maintained and the headmasters of the schools and other teachers were consulted as to the type of broadcasts that would be of interest and benefit to the school-going population.

Hostels for Residential and Day-Residential Schools

We have recommended both residential schools and day-residential schools. Residential schools should provide for accommodation not merely for the pupils but also for some of the teachers. There should also be enough of open space for playgrounds for the residential schools. In the design of residential schools, proper accommodation should be provided for library, for indoor games, dinning halls, dormitories and separate accommodation for the care and isolation of the sick. The care of the sick in residential schools, is a responsibility of the management and while efforts may be made to admit those who are seriously sick in the neighbouring hospitals for minor ailments, arrangements for temporary isolation should be provided.

We have already referred to that fact that in the day-residential schools children would be expected to come in the morning and stay there till late in the evening and that through the cafeteria or otherwise, arrangements may be made to provide them with mid-day meals and refreshments at cheap rates. It is therefore necessary that there should be a dining room for the purpose and also certain common rooms where the pupils may take rest. In this connection we wish to stress the need for a cafeteria to be opened in all day schools. It is unfortunate that the managements have not taken care that their school children should have, when necessary, clean food and filtered water to drink. We have noticed that several coffee hotels have a brisk trade just by the side of the school, where there is no guarantee of wholesome food or drinks being available.

It should be the endeavour of the managements to see that such shops are not encouraged and that in the school itself a, well run cafeteria providing clean and whole-some food at comparatively cheap rate is available.

We recommend also that cooperative stores be established in all schools providing school requirements at almost the cost price. We feel sure that if the teachers take some interest there should be no difficulty in establishing such cooperative stores. In some States cooperation has a strong hold. The school design should naturally take note of the requirements of cafeteria and cooperative stores.

Quarters for the School Staff

It has not often been realised that for efficient service in the school, the teachers concerned should have suitable quarters as near the school as possible. This is particularly true of schools situated in urban areas. We feel that the presence of the headmaster and some at least of the staff in or near a school, particularly if there are hostels attached or where the schools are residential will be of the greatest, benefit to the school-going population. It will attract teachers to the schools and it will be of great benefit to the management itself if, quarters can be assured. We consider that this is particularly necessary, and not merely desirable, in the case of girls' schools for women teachers. We have had occasion to note that for lack of suitable quarters, there has been great difficulty in recruiting women teachers to some of the girls' schools.

The community life of the teaching staff thus encouraged by the provision of quarters in the area would go a long way to promote their sustained interest in the school and their united effort for the better running of the instituion. We recommend also that quarters should be provided for the teaching staff of boys' schools particularly in rural areas where no quarters are available at present for the majority of the teachers. In urban areas, the cost of rented buildings is prohibitive and teachers with small emoluments can hardly live in decent quarters. We therefore recommend that quarters be also provided as far as possible in the urban areas. In doing so, the State should come to the aid of the schools by starting coopratíve housing societies and by giving loans to the managements of the schools on easy terms. If these recommendations are accepted and adopted, we feel sure that the whole atmosphere of the school will be different, and that efficiency and discipline will improve and the community itself will beg-in to realise that the school is an institution calculated to serve the need not only of the pupils but of the whole community.

Hours of Work and Vacations

In most States the hours of work in schools are specified and a uniform practice is observed which does not take into consideration the varying needs of the locality, the climatic conditions therein and the manner in which the school pupils may best serve their families, we feel considerable latitude, should be, given to schools to arrange their school hours in such a way that they do not interfere with the life of the community or with the, general conditions Prevailing therein. Provided the total number of working days and the number of working hours per day be fixed it should be possible for schools, with the previous approval of the Director to vary the hours of school work, with due, reference to the changes in the season. Particular note may be taken of the requirements of rural schools and of the occupations of the community. Thus during the agricultural seasons when the parents have to depend on the help of their children, it is good for the children to be associated with such occupations of their parents, whatever may be their future vacation in life. Nor do we consider it desirable to have fixed hours common to all schools independently of Seasonal variations

We recommend that the total number of working days in a school should not be less than 200, that the working hours per week be at least 35 periods of 45 minutes each inclusive of time spent for some, of the co-curricular activities of the school. The school should Work regularly for 6 days in the week, one of the days being a half day when the teachers and taught may devote special attention to the pursuit of extra-curricular activities. We have already stated that all teachers should take part in one or other of the extra-curricular activities and with this end in view we recommend that a teacher should not be given more than 30 periods a week.

Vacation and Holidays

No country, perhaps enjoys as many holidays as India and with the innumerable holidays given for various religious functions, the work of the school is seriously handicapped. School work suffers much by interruption and it is far better to give short vacations during the academic year. We recommend that school holidays need not conform to holidays declared by the government, that two months' vacations should be given in summer and that there should be two breaks of 10 to 15 days at suitable occasions in the year.

Recruitment to Public Services

Effect of the Present Method of the Recruitment on Education

We have discussed at considerable length that universities have had a dominating influence on Secondary education which only aims at qualifying candidates for entrance to a university. But more than this, the present method of recruitment to public services in the country has a deadening influence on both Secondary education and other grades of education. Complaints are common that the type of education prevalent for over a hundred years was mainly intended to provide clerks for government service.

Whatever may have been the motives in the past it is obvious that the present and in the future the very large number of young men who seek educational opportunities can never hope to secure employment in government service, because the number of posts is very limited. If education is, to lead the individual to secure employment on the basis of his general accomplishment. it seems necessary that there should be a change not only in the nature of education but also in the policy and in the methods adopted for recruitment to public services.

Present Method of Selection to Services

At present the Public Service Commission holds a competitive test for selecting candidates for different grades of public services. The maximum age for recruitment to most of the services irrespective of the nature of the work is 25 years.

In the case of persons belonging to some of the educationally backward communities there is a relaxation of the age period. It is surprising that the competitive tests for even the lowest grade of clerical posts is based upon this maximum age period and not on the stage of education completed. Both the products of school and of the university are allowed to sit for the same competitive test conducted by the Public Service Commission and it is not clear how the same type of question can hold good for matriculates as well as graduates. It is also difficult to understand how by such a test the achievements of candidates of different grades of education can be evaluated. A boy is thus forced to pursue higher courses of study even up to the age of 25 in the vain hope that, somehow or other, at some period of his educational career he may be able to secure through a competitive test the coveted post of a lower division clerk. Economic wastage involved in this method of recruitment as well as the psychological wastage involved in the unnecessary pursuit of higher academic studies by the unsuitable candidates are obvious. The over-crowding of educational institutions in the higher spheres of education is one of its consequences.

Recruitment in India

In India the usual practice is to recruit persons who are below 25 for all grades and classes of employment and later to leave it to them, in some manner or other, and without any guidance to pass the special tests which are needed for promotion from one post to a higher post.

There is also another unfortunate trend which has come to force in recent years. Promotion to a higher post is based not on his work or the special tests passed by him but on his qualifying for a degree. This has resulted in a constant pressure upon universities to permit employees in government service, to appear for university examinations after private study and obtain a higher qualification.

Methods of Recruitment in Other Countries

We have examined the methods of recruitment in other countries and the principles on which such recruitment is based. The policy in recruitment to the civil services in general and to the administrative posts in particular in the United Kingdom is based upon certain considerations such as:

(i) Recruitment at an early age.

(ii) A close linking of the various methods and stages of entrance with the educational system of the country.

(iii) The emphasis on a general rather than specific preparation for career as an officer.

(v) An examination which does not seek unduly to influence the general school and university curriculum.

(v) Finally as a corollary to the former the desire that candidates who have failed in the civil service tests should not be at a disadvantage in their study for other professions. A general education which enlarges and strengthens their understanding is what is required so that it will precede the special education which must qualify persons to discharge the business of their post.

Suggestions for Improving the Methods of Selection

We believe that to get the most suitable persons for the different grades, the practice that obtains in most of the Western countries should be followed. Selection should be made at various age periods 16 to 18, 19 to 21 and 22 to 24. If the first recruitment is at the age periods of 16 to 18 and a competitive examination is held the person so selected will have received sufficient education and be sufficiently mature for his work and for further training to discharge the particular duties thereof. It should be left to the department concerned to plan the method of, further training for the type of work that is expected. Such training should be given as part of the routine duties he has to perform.

The next category will be those who have attained the age of about 19. That bulk of such candidates are likely to have passed the Higher Secondary stage of examination and would know how to prepare for such a test. Likewise at the next higher age level, the test being of a more advanced nature, it will generally draw candidates who have either completed the university degree or who are appearing for it. This would also give scope for persons who have not the resources to go to colleges but may study privately to compete for selection to administrative posts. People who will be selected for the last grade, between the ages of 22 and 24, will be for highest services like the Indian Administrative or Foreign Service etc. In practice most of them would have obtained a university degree but this should not be put down as sine qua non for appearing for the competitive test.

It may be argued that the number of people who would appear for such a test may be so large that it may not be possible for the Public Service Commission to conduct these examinations. This is no doubt a difficulty but the method has certain definite advantages. The students will not pursue a purposeless education to obtain a degree which would only lead to the over-crowding of colleges by unsuitable candidates and to increase the number of unemployed graduates. Another advantage would be that those who have taken to highly specialised courses of instruction would not then be crowding into government posts for which such training is not needed. It has been rightly pointed out by many leaders of public opinion that the qualifications prescribed for government service in this country have given undue importance to university degrees and this has led to a large number of unfit persons flocking to the universities much to the detriment of standards and the tone of university education. The policy pursued by government in this respect is followed by some employers also.

We therefore recommend that a careful study should be made of the conditions of recruitment and that a university degree should be prescribed only for such posts largely professional-where high academic attainments are obviously necessary.

We recommend that the whole system of recruitment to publicservice should be examined de novo by a competent committee specially appointed to see tow far the methods of recruitment can be improved and how they could be best applied to the different levels of education.

We also recommend that for a transitional period the methods of recruitment that we have suggested based on the age limit should be tried for about 50 per cent of posts while the recruitment to the rest be made on the present basis. The results of these methods should be carefully watched before all the posts are treated on a uniform basis.

2

Education in India

Education has always been accorded an honoured place in the Indian society. The great leaders of Indian freedom movement realised the fundamental role of education and throughout the national struggle for independence stressed its unique significance for national development. The development of education in India during the post-Independence period has been guided by the national goals and aspirations as embodied in the Indian Constitution. Education being a powerful instrument of social, economic and political change, its broad principles and objectives are related to the long-term national goals, the programme of national development on which the country is engaged and the complex shortterm problems it is called upon to solve.

The adoption of the 1968 Policy, which was based on the recommendations of the Education Commission, marked a significant step in the history of education in post Independence India. Since then there has been a considerable expansion in the educational facilities all over the country at all levels. While several prominent educational institutions were established in different parts of the country, particular attention was paid to the creation of basic educational facilities in the rural areas. Efforts were also initiated to adopt a common structure of education throughout the country and to lay down a common scheme of studies for boys and girls.

While these achievements were impressive by themselves. the general formulations incorporated in the 1968 Policy neither, got translated into a detailed strategy of implementation nor, were accompanied by the assignment of specific responsibilities and financial and organisational support. Problems of access, quantity, quality, relevance and financial outlay, as a result, accumulated over the years.

It was in response to this that the new National Policy on Education (NPE) was adopted in May, 1986 after a comprehensive appraisal of the existing educational scenario. The Policy laid great emphasis on developing a national system of education, the elimination of disparities in the educational system and provision of more facilities through qualitative interventions. It proposed to decentralise educational administration with a view to make it more responsive to the needs of the people.

One of the significant aspects of the NPE, 1986 is the greater concern for the empowerment of women, and access to education to disadvantaged sections of the society, educationally backward minorities and the disabled. The Policy gave added impetus to the launching of a largescale programme of non-formal education, boldly acknowledging that the school system cannot reach all children. In order to nurture rural talent, the establishment of Navodaya Vidyalayas (model schools) with residential facilities, was also part of the NPE, 1986. It also called for greater rigour and discipline in academic pursuits, autonomy and accountability, experimentation and innovation, nurture of excellence and modernisation of processes at different levels of education.

The NPE, 1986. in consonance with the earlier Policy, also proposed that the implementation of its various parameters be reviewed every five years. It also called for appraisals at short intervals to "ascertain the progress of implementation and the trends emerging from time to time." Accordingly, a review of the 1986 Policy was conducted during 1990-92. The review broadly endorsed the National Policy on Education. Based on an in-depth review of the whole gamut of educational situation and formulated on the basis of national consensus, the NPE enunciated a comprehensive framework to guide the development of education in its entirity.

While that framework continues to be of relevance, the development during the last few years and the experience gained in the implementation of the Policy had necessitated certain modifications. These modifications were introduced in May, 1992. Universalisation of elementary education, equalisation of educational opportunities, women's education and development, vocationalisation of secondary education, consolidation of higher education, modernisation of technical education, improvement of quality, content and process of education at all levels continue to be the themes of national endeavour in the field of education.

One of the significant changes is that the focus in elementary education has now shifted from enrolment, per se, to retention and achievement. The revised Policy resolves to ensure "that free and compulsory education of satisfactory quality is provided to all children upto 14 years of age before we enter the twenty-first century." In order to achieve this a national mission is proposed to be launched for the achievement of this goal. In fact, the experience of the National Literacy Mission has proved that the mission mode is the most effective strategy for achieving total literacy. The total literacy campaigns will be the means for achieving total adult literacy. The revised policy formulations have also extended the scope of vocational education by including generic vocational courses.

Consequent on revision of the Policy, the Government also prepared a revised Programme of Action (POA) in August, 1992. The POA, 1992 emphasises that the first and the foremost task is to reform the management of education and calls for developing an ethos of cost-effectiveness and accountability at all levels of educational planning and administration. It advocates that efficiency should be rated not by the ability to consume budget and demand more but by performance and delivery. The POA envisages preparation of action plans at the state and district levels in tune with the situational imperative.

The POA, as mentioned above, calls for launching a national mission to ensure the achievement of universalisation of elementary education by the year 2000 as set out in the modified Policy. It has also proposed alternative channels of schooling like voluntary schools and non-formal education centres for those who cannot attend conventional full-time schools. It has suggested improvement of facilities in schools through revamped Operation Blackboard to be extended to upper primary stage. The POA notes that the total literacy campaign has emerged as a viable model. It has transformed the perception of universal adult literacy from one of the hopeless dreams to an achievable prospect.

The POA perceives the problem of universalisation of elementary education as, in essence, the problem of the girl child and stresses the need to increase participation of girls at all stages of education, particularly in streams like science, vocational, technical and commerce education where girls are grossly under-rated. The POA stresses the need for reorienting the education system to promote women's equality and education. It advocates need for institutional mechanism to ensure that gender sensitivity is reflected in the implementation of all national programmes. It also calls for curbing the unplanned proliferation of sub-standard institutions.

EDUCATIONAL PLANNING

The Constitution of India places Education in the concurrent list. The NPE 1986 explains the concept of concurrency as a meaningful partnership involving "a new sharing of responsibility between the Union Government and the States in respect of this vital area of national life. This concept enables the Centre and the States to make concerted efforts for the development of education maintaining a broad uniformity in standards and structures.

Educational planning in the country is essentially the joint endeavour of the Central and the State Governments. The Planning Commission at the Centre and the State Planning Departments decide the policy and approach to be adopted. At the Central level a planning and monitoring division in the Department of Education (DOE) works in close liaison with the education division of the Planning Commission.

Actions related to education at the national level including planning and policy-making are guided and coordinated by the Central Advisory Board of Education (CABE), the members of which include Ministers of Education of all States and Union Territories and leading educationists of the country. A few national level institutions specialising in particular aspects of education, assist and advise the Central and State Governments in the formulation and implementation of policies and programmes in their respective areas. Special mention may be made in this regard, of organisations such as the National Institute of Educational Planning and

Administration, the National Council of Educational Research and Training and the University Grants Commission.

Organisation and Structure of the Education System

Decisions regarding the organisation and structure of education are largely the concern of the States. Within the overall policy framework, each State independently determines the educational structure to be adopted, particularly at the school stage.

Some variations can be found in the educational structure within the school stage.The primary and upper primary or middle stages together constitute the elementary stage. It has been envisaged that there should be a common structure for the elementary stage consisting of 5 years of primary schooling followed by 3 years of upper primary/middle school education. It is visualised that the States where the first ten years are divided into four years of primary, three years of upper primary and three years of secondary schooling, will attempt to switch over to 5+3+2 pattern by 1995. At present, corresponding to the number of years spent at the elementary stage, the secondary stage consists of 2 to 3 years of schooling which marks the completion of the ten years of general education programme.

After the age of 14 years, a child can either join the secondary school providing general education programmes or alternatively a voca-tional school or an Industrial Training Institute which equips her/him with specialised vocational skills. A person who completes 10 years of general education has similar choice either to take up academic courses at the higher secondary level preparing to join collegiate education or opt for vocational streams within the higher secondary programme or through specialised institutions such as

Polytechnics and Industrial Training Institutes. Completion of higher secondary education qualifies the individual for entering first degree programmes. Admission to professional courses such as engineering and medicine, at this stage, is highly competitive. Even demand for admission to different programmes in arts, science and commerce fields vary considerably.

Demographic Composition

The population of India has been growing steadily over the past several decades. The growth rate has been higher particularly after 1951. The total population figures according to census are presented in Table 1.

Table 1

Growth of Population

Census Year	*Total population (In Millions)*	*Growth rate*
1951	361	+13.31
1961	439	+21.64
1971	548	+24.80
1981	683	+24.66
1991	844	+23.50

Literacy

The sex-wise literacy rates (percentage) related to population aged five years and above as per the various population census from 1951 onwards are given in Table 2.

As is observed from Table 2, the literary rates have shown a considerable increase since independence. However one glaring fact is that there still exists a considerable disparity between the male and female literacy rates.

Institutions and Coverage

During the period between 1950-51 and 1990-91, the number of primary and upper primary level institutions grew from 223 thousand to about 705 thousand, registering more than a three-fold increase (Table 3). In terms of the overall growth rate, the increase was to the tune of 2.48 per cent for primary level and 6.13 percent for upper primary level institutions.

Table 2. Literacy Rates

Year	*Persons*	*Males*	*Females*
1951	18.33	27.16	8.86
1961	28.31	40.40	15.34
1971	34.45	45.95	21.97
1981	43.56	56.37	29.75
	(41.42)	(53.45)	(28.46)
1991	52.11	63.86	39.42

Table 3. Growth of Recognised Educational Institutions Since 1951

Institutions	*Years* 1950-51	1960-61	1970-71	1980-81	1990-91
Primary	209671	330399	408378	494503	558392
Upper Primary	13596	49663	90621	118355	146636
High/Hr.Sec. Schools/Inter. Pre-Degree/Jr. Colleges.	7416	17329	37051	51624	78619
College for Ge. Education	370	967	2285	3421	4862
Colleges for Prof.					

Education	208	852	992	1156	886
Universities	27	45	82	110	146

Table 2 and 3 illustrate the above table. During the eighties the growth rates of primary and upper primary level institutions work out to be 1.2 per cent and 2.2 per cent, respectively. Educational institutions at all levels except the primary level, registered higher growth rates in the eighties than in the seventies. The slow growth of primary level institutions can possibly be attributed to the fact that a significant level of coverage of population had already been achieved by 1980.

Those habitations which are not covered by a formal school, have other modes of imparting education (NFE and the Open School System). The number of non-formal centres in 1988-89 was 241 thousand. Each centre is expected to operate with an enrolment of about 30 children.

Enrolment and Retention

In terms of growth of enrolment, the period since 1947 could be divided into two phases. The first phase corresponds to the period beginning with the fifties and ending with the seventies. It was characterised by the gradual slowing down of growth rates. The second phase corresponds to the eighties, characterised by an upswing in enrolment coverage.

For primary education, the annual growth rate for the fifties was 6.2 per cent which declined to 5.0 per cent in the sixties and 2.6 per cent in the seventies.

During the eighties, however, the enrolment growth rates increased to 3.0 per cent. Beginning with 1980-81 and up to 1990-91 the data indicate a siginficant increase in enrollments at all levels. This is more pronounced at the secondary level, followed by upper primary and primary levels respectively, indicative of the intensity of the thrust, resulting from the expanding base of the educational hierarchy.

The Scheduled Caste (SC) and the Scheduled Tribe (ST) population is generally compared to those joining the upper primary level. Consequently, the current backlog continues to increase. This is clearly indicated by the divergence between primary and upper primary enrolment trends in the data.

Table 4. Enrolment of Students at Different Levels of School Education

(In 000's)

Year	*Primary Upper*	*Primary*	*High/Hr. Sec*
1950-51	19,154	3,120	1,441
1960-61	34,994	6,705	3,345
1970-71	57,045	13,315	7,600
1980-81	73,774	20,724	11,871
1990-91	99,118	33,283	20,897

It may be noted that enrolment figures as discussed above are based on gross enrolment, which includes underage and overage children. It is expected that as the size of enrolment increases, the share of underage and overage children in the total enrolment which is estimated to be around 25 per cent will decrease and consequently the enrolment figures will become more realistic. belonging to these communities at different levels of school education.

The efficiency of an education system is determined not only by enrolling more and more but also by ensuring their retention in the system. Cohortwise analysis shows that out of 100 students enrolled in Class I in 1951, only 33 could be retained up to Class V. However, the retention rates have tended to improve with time. From the latest data available i.e. for the year 1987-88, it has been estimated that enrolment in Grade V is 53 per cent of the enrolment in Grade I.

Teachers

In terms of the number of teachers, a substantial increase has been registered from 1950-51 to 1990-91 as may be seen from Table 5.

The increase in the number of teachers took place across all levels of education. In the primary stage their number grew from about 0.54 million in 1950-51 to about 1.6 million in 1990-91. (a growth of 2.8 per cent per annum). During the same period the number of teachers at the upper primary level increased from 0.09 million to 1.06 million with an overall growth rate of 6.5 percent per annum.

1.32 The national average of pupil-teacher ratio at the primary level increased from 39 in 1971-72 to 42 in 1990-91. A similar increase was also witnessed in the case of the upper primary level. The growth in the number of secondary teachers was modest as compared to the increase in enrolments at that level.

Financing of Education

A quick glance at the trends in public expenditure on education shows that over the years, the percentage of GNP spent on education has been increasing. At the inception of planning (1950-51) (Table 6). While the increase is significant, the actual requirements of the system exceed the present provisions. The view put forth by the Education Commission (1964-66) that the public expenditure on education should be 6 per cent of the GNP has been reiterated time and again by various committees and commissions and has become a national resolve. The NPF states that "during the Eighth Five Year

Table 5. Distribution of Teachers by Type of Schools since 1951

(In 000's)

	Year		*Primary*				*Upper Primary*		*High*
		Male	*Female*	*Total*	*Male*	*Female*	*Total*	*Male*	*Female*
Total									
1950-51	456	82	538	73	13	86	107	**20**	127
1960-61	615	127	742	262	83	**345**	234	62	296
1970-71	835	225	1060	463	175	**638**	474	155	629
1980-81	020	343	1363	598	253	851	658	254	912
1990-91	1167	470	1637	706	353	1059	857	416	1273

Plan and onwards it will uniformly exceed 6 per cent of the National Income."

Table 6. Share of Education in GNP

Percy)

Years	*Share of Education*
1950-51	1.2
1960-61	2.5
1970-71	3.1
1980-81	3.1
1989-90	3.9

The emphasis during the first two decades after independence was on building up an infrastructural and institutional base for the development of education in the coming decades. This had resulted in a higher percentage of expenditure on higher and technical education in the initial years after independence. Once this infrastructure has been built up, the efforts have shifted towards widening the access and improving the quality of elementary education which is perceived as a minimum need, This shift is more conspicuous after 1986.

Two significant development have taken place since NPE, 1986 was enunciated. In line with the principle of concurrency enshrined in the Constitution, the Central Government's share in expenditure on elementary and adult education has increased. The share of the Centre in the expenditure on elementary education increased from 11.7 percent in Sixth Five Year Plan to 22.6 per cent in Seventh Five Year Plan and to 38.7 percent in Eighth Five Year Plan. This is because a number of new schemes intended to enhance the access to education and to improve the quality, such as Operation Blackboard. were initiated. There has also been a remarkable shift in the, inter se, allocation of public resources for education. The outlay on elementary education increased from 33.0 per cent in the Sixth Plan to 37.33 per cent in the Seventh Plan and to 46.95 per cent in the Eighth Plan. Conversely, the shares of higher and technical education have been steadily declining during this period. The expenditure on higher education which was 22.09 percent in the Sixth Plan declined to 15,74 per cent in the Seventh Plan. The outlay for this sector in the Eighth Plan forms only 7.73 percent. The corresponding figures for technical education are 10.79, 14.19 and 14.22 per cent respectively. This trend is evident not only in the Central Government's expenditure but in that of the State Governments too.

Another important facet of expenditure on education which the POA, 1992 has highlighted is the increased strees on cost-effectiveness. It is increasingly being realised that "Progress should cease to be driven by budgets and instead should stress process and outcomes; efficiency should be rated not by the ability to consume budget and demand more but by the performance and delivery." There is an emerging consensus that the failure to achieve Universalisation of Elementary Education is more due to systemic deficiencies than due to resources per se. The systemic deficiencies are being remedied to ensure better cost effectiveness.

3

National Policy on Education: Trends and Perspectives

The Government of India, in August this year brought out a detailed plan of action entitled 'Programme of Action, 1992' (POA) translating the National Policy on Education, 1986 as modified in 1992, into concrete action points.

Early Childhood Care and Education

The National Policy on Education (NPE) has given a great deal of importance to Early Childhood Care mid Education (ECCE). It views ECCE as a crucial input in the strategy of human resource development (HRD), as a feeder and support programme for primary education and as a support service for working women of the disadvantaged sections of the society. It has also taken into account the holistic nature of ECCE and has pointed out the need for organising programmes for the all-round development of the child. It specifically focusses on the need for early care and stimulation of children belonging to the vulnerable sections of the society. Since the age span covered by ECCE is from conception to 6 years, emphasis has been given to a child centred approach, play way and activity based learning in place of formal methods of teaching and early introduction of the three R's. The importance of community involvement has also been highlighted. Emphasis has been given to establishing linkages between Integrated Child Development Service (ICDS) and other ECCE programmes. The Revised Policy Formulations reiterate the postulates of NPE, 1986 on ECCE.

The existing ECCE programmes include:

(i) ICDS.

(ii) Scheme of assistance to voluntary organisations for conducting Early Childhood Education (ECE) centres.

(iii) Balwadis and day-care centres run by voluntary agencies with Government's assistance.

(iv) Pre-primary schools run by the State Governments, Municipal Corporations and other governmental and non-governmental agencies.

(v) Material and child health services through primary health centres, subcentres and other agencies.

ICDS is currently the biggest programme of early childhood development, with 290 thousand Anganwadis serving nearly 14 million children and about 2.7 million mothers; 91.5 per cent ICDS projects are located in rural and tribal areas and 8.5 percent in urban slums. Besides the ICDS, by the end of 1991-92, there were 12,470 creches with a coverage of about 300 thousand children below 5 years, 4395 ECE centres in 9 Educationally Backward(EB) States and the Balwadi Nutrition Programme serving nearly 230 thousand children in the age-group of 3-5 years. The aim of ECCE is dig every child should be assured access to the fulfilment of all basic needs. As such efforts will be made towards universalisation of ICDS by A.D. 2000.

Over the recent years, a number of initiatives have been taken to make the programmes more specific. These inter alia, include training for the personnel, revision of the content of the programmes, provision of adequate instructional and play materials and enlisting community and parental participation wherever possible in resource mobilisation, planning and implementation.

Elementary Education

Provision of free and compulsory education to all children until they complete the age of 14 years is a Directive Principle of the Constitution of India. Since 1950 determined efforts have been made towards the achievement of this goal. Over the years there has been an impressive increase in the number and spread of institutions as well as enrolment rates. Universal provision of institutions has been substantially achieved at the primary stage (classes IN). According to the Fifth AR India Educational Survey (1986), 94.5 per cent of the rural population had primary schools/sections within a walking distance of 1 Km. and 83.98 per cent of the rural population was served with middle schools/sections within a walking distance of 3 Km. As seen from Similarly, the number of upper primary schools went upto 147 thousand in 1990-91 as compared to 13,600 in 1950-51. The gross enrolment ratio for children in age group 6-11 years increased from 43.1 per cent in 1950-51 to 62.4 per cent in 1960-61 to 76.4 per cent in 1970-71 to 80.5 per cent in 1980-81 and to 101 per cent in 1990-91. Likewise, the gross enrolment of 11-14 age group increased from 12.9 percent in 1950-51 to 22.5 percent in 1960-61 to 33.4 per cent in 1970-71 to 41.9 per cent in 1980-81 and to 60 percent in 1990-91.

However, Universalisation of Elementary Education (UEE) in its totality is still an elusive goal and much ground is yet to be covered. Dropout rates continue to be significant. retention of children in schools is low and wastage considerable. In 1987-88, drop-out rates were 46.97 per cent in classes IN and 62.29 per cent in classes I-VIII. Despite increased participation of girls, disparity still exists. Though the participation of girls in primary education (classes IN) increased from 28.1 per cent in 1950-51 to 41.4 percent in 1990-91, it was still below the normative percentage of about 50 per cent. The participation of girls in upper primary classes (classes VI-VIII) was lower, it increased from 16.1 per cent in 1950-51 to 37.4 per cent in 1990-91. The participation of SCs and STs is now more or less in proportion to their share in population at the primary level, but the sex disparity persists among SCs and STs. In classes IN, SC girls account for 38.4 percent of SC students and in classes VI-VIII 33.9 per cent. The corresponding percentages of ST girls are 37.0 per cent and 33.9 per cent respectively.

The NPE, 1986, and its POA gave unqualified priority to UEE and introduced many innovations.First,the emphasiswasshiftedfrom enrolment per se to enrolment as well as retention. As the POA, 1986 put it crisply "enrolment by itself is of little importance if children do not continue beyond one year, many of them not seeing the school for more than a few days." Secondly, the NPE, 1986 sought to adopt an array of meticulously formulated strategies based on micro-planning, and applied at the grass root level all over the country, to ensure children's retention at school. POA, 1986 sought to replace enrolment drives by participative planning in which the teachers and the villagers would formulate family-wise and child-wise design of action to ensure that every child regularly attended school or non-formal education centre and completed at least five years of schooling or its nonformal equivalent. Thirdly, the NPE, 1986 recognised that unattractive school environment, unsatisfactory condition of buildings and insufficiency of instructional material function as demotivating factors for children and their parents. The Policy, therefore, called for a drive for a substantial improvement of primary schools and provision of support services. The scheme of Operation Blackboard was conceived to meet this challenge.The launching of this scheme has greater significance in that it was a manifestation of the Union's intent to shoulder its sham of responsibilities in this vital area of national life, a responsibility arising from Education being in the Concurrent List. Fourthly, the NPE, 1986 commended the adoption at the primary stage of a child-centred and activity-based process of learning. Fifthly, the NPE, 1986 and its POA postulated a large programme of restructuring of teacher education, pre-service as well as in-service.

Table 1. Gross Enrolment Ratio

		1986-87	*1990-91*
Total Enrolment			
Classes I-V	Girls	79.21	85.97
	Total	95.96	101.03
Classes VI-VIII	Girls	38.95	46.13
	Total	53.14	60.11
SC Enrolment			
Classes I-V	Girls	64.8	80.6
	Total	84.8	102.2
Classes VI-VIII	Girls	26.5	33.3
	Total	40.0	47.7
ST Enrolment			
Classes I-V	Girls	68.0	78.6
	Total	90.1	103.3
Classes VI-VIII	Girls	21.9	27.5
	Total	34.1	39.7

Last but the most important, the NPE, 1986 sought to address the most difficult aspect of access, viz., access to education for millions of girls and working children who, because of socioeconomic compulsions, cannot participate in school system. As rightly pointed out by the NPERC, it was for the first time, in 1986, that an educational policy had admitted that the school would not reach all children and that a large and systematic programme of Non-Formal Education (NFE) has to be an integral component of the strategy to achieve UEE. NFE, as envisaged by the NPE, 1986 and its POA, would have enough flexibility to enable the learners to learn at their own pace and at the same time would have quality comparable with formal education.

Most of the directives of NPE and POA, 1986 have been operationalised by the Union and States/UTs. The number of primary schools has increased from 529 thousand in 1985-86 to 558 thousand in 1990-91; and the number of upper primary schools has increased from 135 thousand to 146 thousand during the same period. The Development of Education in India details of the increase in gross enrolment ratios are given in Table 1.

By March, 1992, Operation Blackboard covered 414 thousand (77%) schools in 5385 (84%) Community Development Blocks and 1142 (29%) Municipal areas. Owing to resource constraint all the primary schools of the country could not be covered as envisaged. About 70,000 (46%) teachers have been appointed as against 152 thousand single teacher schools identified for coverage. Over 100 thousand (43%) class rooms have been constructed as against the target of 239 thousand.

Following the guidelines in the National Curricular Framework, the National Council of Educational Research and Training (NCERT) revised the entire school syllabi and brought out revised textbooks for classes I to XII. Based on the National Curricular Framework and the

NCERT syllabi/textbooks, the States have also undertaken measures of curriculum renewal and development of new textbooks for different stages of school education for their introduction into the school system in a phased manner.

Guidelines for operationalising microplanning have been prepared and distributed to the State Governments. The concept of micro-planning and local level capacity building have been given currency and efforts launched to decentralise educational planning and management vide new schemes or experimental projects. The resulting impact of these measures is expected to be felt during the coming years.

A positive externality, rather unanticipated, of the Total Literacy Campaigns, has been that in many districts covered by the campaign an upsurge in the demand for primary education is noticeable. In quite a few districts "out of school" children in the age group 9-14 were covered by the campaigns. Further, in these districts the awareness generated among parents is leading to better participation of children in primary schools. This pleasant experience has reconfirmed the need to pay more attention to the "demand side" in strategies for achieving UEE and highlighted the need for a disaggregated approach to the problem of UEE whereby districts, not States, and specific disadvantaged groups the girls of SCs and STs should become the basis for future planning.

Significant developments have taken place in the area of learner achievement. The NPE, 1986 spells out the Minimum Levels of Learning (MLL) and states that "to promote equality it will be necessary to provide equal opportunity to all not only in access but also in the condition for success. Besides, awareness of the inherent equality of all will be created through the core curriculum. Minimum Levels of Learning will be laid down for each stage of education." In pursuance of this policy and based on the report of a Committee appointed by the Ministry of HRD in 1990 and the recommendations of the Central Advisory Board of Education (CABE), MLL have been laid down for the primary stage with the intention of reducing the curriculum load and making it more relevant and functional for those children who have no support for learning at home or outside the school, who are not likely to avail of the opportunity of education beyond this stage and who must learn here what is required to sustain them throughout their lives and enable them to function in their world as socially useful and contributing individuals. It is now acknowledged that UEE cannot be accepted as having been achieved unless children passing out of school acquire MLL. Achievement has come to be assigned equal importance alongwith access and retention.

Another important development was the World Conference on Education for All (EFA) held in March 1990, in Jomtien, Thailand. The Conference was organised by UNESCO, UNICEF, UNDP and the World Bank and attended by 155 member states of United Nations and several donor agencies. The Conference adopted a declaration calling upon all member states and international agencies to take effective steps for achieving EFA by the year A.D. 2000. The Conference advocated a holistic concept of basic education in lieu of a pectoral approach segregating sections like Primary Schooling, Non-formal Education, Adult and Continuing Education in separate compartments. In order to hamess increased donor interest in the basic education, as a result of the Conference, it was decided to formulate comprehensive basic education projects in educationally backward States.

The failure to universalise elementary education and literacy is not only a question of lack of resources but also of systemic deficiencies. The additional resources that may be available under external assistance should, therefore, be used for educational reconstruction which should go beyond the conventional measures such as opening new schools, construction of school buildings and appointing teachers. It is necessary to adopt a holistic approach, and to address

i) the educational needs of the working children, girls and disadvantaged groups,and

ii) issues of content, process and quality.

Projects should also be used to develop sus-tainable and replicable models in different programmes related to basic education. Therefore, these projects should be developed and implemented in the true spirit of meaningful participation between the Centre and States as envisaged in NPE. It would also be necessary to implement these projects in a mission mode with effective and participative management structures and with involvement of local community, teachers and NGOs.

Two such externally assisted projects, viz., the Bihar Education Project with Unesco assistance and the Lok Jumbish Project in Rajasthan with the assistance of Swedish International Development Agency have been launched. The CABE further decided that project formulation should be a process of capacity building.

While reiterating the priority for UEE as well as the policy frame outlined by NPE, 1986, the Revised Policy Formulations (RPF) brought about following modifications:

i) Achieving essential levels of learning has been specifically incorporated as one of the thrust areas in para 5.5; this is a logical consequence of the increasing importance that came to be attached to MLL alongwith access and retention.

ii) Scope of Operation Blackboard (OB) has been enlarged to provide three reasonably large rooms and three teachers in every primary school; it has also been decided to extend OB to the upper primary stage.

iii) It has been specifically laid down that at least 50 per cent of the teachers recruited in future should be women.

iv) Taking a realistic view of the enormous task of achieving UEE in its entirety (access, retention as well as achievement), the RPF envisage that free and compulsory education of satisfactory quality should be provided to all children upto 14 years of age before the commencement of the twenty-first century.

v) Taking note of the effectiveness of the Mission mode in social sectors, particularly literacy, the RPF envisage launching of a national mission to ensure the achievement of UEE by the year 2000.

In the Eighth Plan the strategy for UEE envisages adoption of disaggregated target setting and decentralised planning. An analysis of the educational indicators reveals that within each State, even in the educationally backward ones, there are areas and districts which are almost within reach of universalisation, while even in the educationally advanced States there are districts which are still quite backward. The attempt, therefore would be to prepare district-specific and population-specific plans for UEE within the broad strategy frame of Microplanning through people's participation and introduction of Minimum Levels of Learning (MLL) in schools to improve learner achievement. Microplanning will provide the framework for universal access and universal participation while MLL would be the strategy frame for universal achievement.

In order to reduce disparities a disaggregated approach will be adopted through district planning by classifying districts into four categories :

i) High literacy districts in which access and enrolment are almost universal and community awareness for education is already high;

ii) Total literacy campaign districts in which community mobilisation for educational needs has been successfully generated by the National Literacy Mission;

iii) Low literacy districts in which the provision of education facilities is unsatisfactory and the delivery system functions without any community involvement; and

iv) Externally assisted project districts with a different management structure and sufficient financial support

The strategies with regard to access, participation, achievement, environment building, community participation, etc. will be different for these four categories of districts.

Under this broad strategy of district planning and based on the experience gained in implementation of NPE, and the RPF, the following strategies are proposed :

i) Adoption of alternative channels of schooling like voluntary schools and NFE centres for those who cannot avail of conventional full-time schooling.

ii) Microplanning through involvement of teachers and the community in order to design and implement a family-wise, child-wise plan of action for universal access/enrolment and participation.

iii) Making parents aware about their responsibility for ensuring the completion of elementary education by their children and for providing at home the facilities and encouragement needed for this purpose.

iv) Establishment of linkages between programmes of pre-school and primary education, and between programmes of literacy and UEE, in total literacy campaign districts.

v) Improvement of school facilities through revamped Operation Blackboard and connecting it to MLL strategy. It will also be extended to upper primary stage.

vi) Decentralisation of educational management for making the schools function so as to ensure universal enrolment, retention and achievement.

vii) Introduction of MLLs at primary and upper primary stages including coverage of the non-formal education channel.

viii) Revision of process and content of elementary education to make teaching-learning child centred, activity based and joyful.

ix) Introduction of continuous and comprehensive evaluation with focus on remedial measures.

x) Modification of teacher training programmes in view of changed strategies and programmes.

xi) Improvement of the monitoring system for UEE.

xii) Launching a National Mission to achieve the goals envisaged in the revised Policy.

Further efforts would be made to develop district specific projects, with specific activities, clearly defined responsibilities, definite timeschedule and specific targets. Each district project will be prepared within the major strategy framework and will be tailored to the specific needs and possibilities in the district. Apart from effective UEE, the goals of each project will include the reduction of existing disparities in educational access, the provision of alternative systems of comparable standards to the disadvantaged groups, a substantial improvement in the quality of schooling facilities, obtaining a genuine community involvement in the running of schools, and building up local level capacity to ensure effective decentralisation of educational planning. That is to say, the overall goal of the project would be reconstruction of primary education as a whole in selected districts instead of a piecemeal implementation of schemes. An integrated approach is more likely to achieve synergies among different programme components.

Non-formal Education

The role of non-formal part-time education in providing education to working children, and children in habitations without schools has been recognised since the Education Commission of 1964-66. During 1979-80, the scheme of Non-Formal Education (NFE) was introduced as an alternative strategy to impart education to children, who for various reasons cannot attend formal schools. The NPE envisaged a large and systematic programme of NFE to achieve UEE. The scheme was revised in its content and emphasis in 1987-88. Although its focus is on the ten educationally backward States, namely, Andhra Pradesh, Arunachal Pradesh, Assam, Bihar, Jammu & Kashmir, Madhya Pradesh, Orissa, Rajasthan, Uttar Pradesh and West Bengal, it has been extended to cover urban slums, hilly, tribal and desert areas and areas with concentration of working children in the other States as well. Financial responsibility is borne by the Central and State Governments in the ratio of 50:50 for general (co-educational) and 90 : 10 for girls NFE centres. Assistance to the extent of 100 per cent is provided to voluntary agencies for running NFE centres and for experimental and innovative projects.

The (revised) NFE scheme has been visualised as child-centred, environmentoriented, flexible system to meet the educational needs of the comparatively deprived geographical areas and socio-economic sections of the society. Other features of the scheme are its organisational flexibility, relevance of curriculum, diversity in learning activities to relate them to the learner's needs and decentralised management. The programme is being implemented on a project basis, generally co-terminus with the community development Block comprising about 100 NFE Centres.

In order to strengthen the NFE Scheme the following strategies are being adopted :

i) Provision of NFE centres will be based on the Microplanning exercise carried out for UEE. NFE centres will invariably cater to the needs of children, especially girls, who are not able to or who cannot attend the formal school.

ii) The community will be involved in ate setting-up, and supervision of all NFE centres.

iii) The NFE instructors will be identified with the help of the community. Special efforts will be made to appoint women instructors wherever possible.

iv) Training of NFE personnel, especially instructors, will be given top priority. Adequate training and reorientation will, be provided.

v) Training responsibility will be shared by the project, District level institutions like DIETs, DRUs, State level institutions like SCERT, and National institutes like NCERT and NIEPA.

vi) Project administration will be strengthened for effective decentralisation of management. Necessary administrative and management inputs will be provided at the State and District levels.

vii) Arrangements will be made for testing of children in the NFE stream with reference to an equivalent Stage in the formal system and specific instructions issued to facilitate lateral entry into the formal system for students of the NFE stream.

viii) Efforts will be made Lo link non-for-mal courses with the Open Schools.

ix) The NFE programme will be linked with the scheme of public libraries, Jana Shiksha Nilayams, etc.

x) In total literacy campaign districts follow-up programmes will be taken up for children in the age-group 9-14 to go beyond NLM literacy norms.This will form apart of the postliteracy and continuing education programme of the district.

xi) Vocational and technical courses of wide variety will be provided for children and youth who pass out of the Non-Formal stream. Shramik Vidyapeeth and Vountary agencies will be involved in this process.

xii) Voluntary agencies will be encouraged to undertake projects of NFE, especially in areas where the formal school system is not able to meet the demands of UEE.

Adult Literacy

The National Literacy Mission (NLM) which was launched on 5th May, 1988, with the objective of imparting functional literacy to 80 million adult illiterates in the age-group 15-35 by 1995 has entered its fifth year of operationalisation.The Mission has confirmed in more than one sense that eradication of illiteracy is not a utopian idea but something which is possible, feasible and achievable. The first positive indication came from the provisional figures of the 1991 census released by the Registrar General and the Census Commissioner of India.

The literacy rate for the population aged 7 and above in the country increased from 43.56 per cent in 1981 to 52.11 per cent in 1991, registering an increase of 8.55 per cent. Whereas the male literacy in creased from 56.37 percent to 66.83 percent, the female literacy increased from 29.7 per cent to 39.42 per cent. For the first time, the country achieved the distinction of having larger number of literate persons (352.00 million) than the illiterate ones (324.00 million).

Several exciting and interesting developments have taken place in the area of literacy and adult education since the launching of National Literacy Mission in 1988 in general and the call for "Education for All" in the Jomtien World Conference held in March, 1990 in particular.

The mass campaign for eradication of illiteracy launched in Eranakulam district of Kerala in 1989, with the active involvement of persons of all walks of life, achieved significant success and the district achieved the distinction of becoming the first fully literate district in the country on 4th February, 1990. Encouraged by this success, Total Literacy Campaigns were launched to cover the entire States of Kerala and Goa and the Union Territory of Pondicherry. At present, 156 districts in the country are covered by the Total Literacy Campaigns either fully or partially. The entire State of Kerala, the Union Territory of Pondicherry, Burdwan and Midnapur districts in West Bengal, Bijapur and South Kannad district in Karnataka, Sindhudurg and Wardha districts in Maharashtra, Puddukottai and P.T.T. Sivaganga districts in Tamil Nadu have already concluded the Total Literacy Campaigns and have achieved success ranging between 65 to 75 per cent. Other campaigns are in different stages of implementation.

The number of students participating in the National Literacy Mission crossed one million by 1991-92. All the other existing programmes were also reviewed and revised to conform to the principle of area approach for total literacy. The thrust areas under the National Literacy Mission include continuous environment building conducive to literacy, use of IPCL (Increased Pace and Content of Learning) materials in all literacy programmes and organisation of mass campaigns for total literacy in a definite timeframe as dominant strategy for eradication of illiteracy in all programmes of adult education.

After experimenting with successive and alternative models of adult literacy, NLM has now settled down to a model which has given lot of hope and faith that illiteracy can be overcome in a time-bound manner with planned and co-ordinated efforts and with mobilisation of all sections of the society. In addition to 156 districts already covered by the Total Literacy Campaigns, 200 additional districts would be covered by such campaigns by the close of 1997-98,

There are certain characteristic features of Total Literacy Campaigns (TLCs) which make them unique in relation to other programmes. These are as under :

i) These campaigns are area-specific, time-bound, volunteer-based, costeffective and outcome oriented.

ii) These am implemented through the District Level Committees which are registered under the Societies Registration Act under the leadership of the District Collector/Chief Secretary, Zila Parishad (District Council). All sections of society are given due representation in the matter of planning and implementation of programmes.

iii) The TLCs cater to both the demand syndrome and the supply mechanism. In other words, a positive demand of the people for literacy is generated first before the delivery mechanism is provided.

iv) A culture of equality is pervasive in a TLCs. It is implemented in the nature of a people's movement which every one owns, where every one contributes and participates.

v) Though the TLC is meant to impart functional literacy it can be at the same time a campaign for the universal enrolment and retention of children in schools, immunisation. propagation of small family norms, protection of maternity and child care, women's equality and empowerment, peace and communal harmony, etc.

vi) Each TLC has a people oriented well-knit management structure at the district, talukas/block, mandal panchayat or village levels. These management committees mostly consist of non-government officials and function in a de-bureaucratised, decentralised and participatory manner which has enabled them to obtain the participation of the people at the grass-root level.

The mass campaign approach is now accepted as a possible achievable and feasible approach. There is now an active and competitive participation of State Governments to take up the TLCs. The District Collectors who were primarily pre-occupied with problems of maintenance of law and order, peace and tranquility and implementation of government funded development programmes and had hardly any acquaintance with the adult education programmes, are now in the vanguard of TLCs and are providing the leadership, motivation, direction and organisational support for these campaigns.

The emphasis in adult literacy programme has completely shifted from mere enrolment of learners in the adult education centres in the traditional centre based approach, to attainment of certain predetermined levels of literacy and numeracy in a given area with a definite time frame. The basic features of this dominant strategy for eradication of illiteracy i.e. they being area-specific, time-bound volunteer-based and result-oriented have been introduced in all other programmes being undertaken for combating illiteracy in the country. Media is being involved in literacy promotion as a tool of dissemination of information, as a tool of mobilisation, motivation and sensitisation, as a tool of learning/sharing information, ideas and experiences, and as a tool of social action for change. Both print and non-print media including the traditional folk art forms are being harnessed in promoting literacy.

Secondary Education

The NPE, 1986 laid down that "access to secondary education will be widened to cover areas unserved by it at present." There has been a significant increase in the number of secondary and higher secondary schools and in enrolment during the period from 1987-88 to 1990-91. During this period enrolment at secondary stage increased by 16.8 per cent and at the higher secondary stage by 17.6 per cent. The number of secondary schools increased from 54,845 in 1987-88 to 59,468 in 1990-91; corresponding figures for higher secondary schools are 16,460 and 19,151 respectively. The ratio of secondary and higher secondary schools to upper primary schools had declined from 1 :1.98 in 1987-88 to 1: 1.86 in 1990-91.

Gender disparities in enrolments are significant. In 1990-91 girls accounted for 33A per cent of the enrolment at the secondary stage and 32 per cent at the higher secondary stage. The SCs and STs also lag behind in regard to enrolment. Thus, SCs account for 11.85 percent at the secondary stage and 9.7 per cent at the higher secondary stage; corresponding figures for STs being 4.21 per cent and 3 per cent respectively.

Though a considerable degree of uniformity has been achieved in regard to common education structure of 10+2+3, there is considerable diversity regarding the location of the +2 stage. In quite a few States it is not part of the school system.

The secondary stage is divided into two very distinct sub-stages -secondary (upto class X) which is the stage of general education and higher secondary (classes XI and XII) which is marked by differentiation and diversification. The national system of education, as stated in the NPE,1986 envisages a National Curricular Framework. Such a framework has already been prepared for the secondary education though its implementation has been uneven. The work of curriculum revision for the secondary stage was undertaken in almost all the States and the Union Territories (UTs). The NCERT also prepared the guidelines, syllabi and textbooks for all stages of school education. For the higher secondary stage, however, the Curricular Framework has not yet been authorised. The NCERT had developed a draft document in 1988 but that document requires to be reviewed keeping in view the emerging concerns. However, several States used the draft National Curricular Framework for the higher secondary stage prepared by the NCERT.

The Revised Policy Formulations take note of the increased demand for secondary education and go beyond NPE, 1986 by calling for a planned expansion of secondary education facilities all over the country. Secondly, they call for higher participation of girls, SCs and STs, particularly in science, vocational and commerce streams. Thirdly, they call for reorganisation of Boards of Secondary Education and vesting them with autonomy "so that their ability to improve the quality of secondary education is enhanced." Fourthly, they envisage that effort will be made to provide computer literacy in as many secondary level institutions as possible so that the children are equipped with necessary computer skills to be effective in the emerging technological world.

Broad parameters of the strategy envisaged include:

— Extending access to secondary education by setting up new schools in the unserved areas and by extending and consolidating the existing facilities, with particular emphasis on ensuring substantially increased enrolment of girls, the SCs and the STs.

— Progressively bringing in the higher secondary stage (and all its equivalents) as a part of the school system in all States.

— Formulating a National Curriculum Framework for the higher secondary stage as well as development of new curricula and instructional packages based on the semester pattern.

— Reviewing and revising the curricula of secondary education (classes IX and X).

— Implementing a comprehensive scheme of examination reform.

— Improving considerably the physical and infrastructural facilities in secondary and higher secondary schools.

— Providing for diversity of courses in higher secondary schools.

— Reviewing afresh the existing system of pre-service teacher education for the secondary stage and formulating and implementing an improved teacher education system.

— Institutionalising in-service teacher training.

— Transforming the role of the Boards of Secondary Education.

— Strengthening the academic institutions and bodies concerned with research and development in the areas of curriculum, instructional materials and equipment for secondary schools.

Vocational Education

The NPE, 1986 advocated a systematic, well-planned programme of vocational education which would be a distinct stream intended to prepare students for identified occupations. It envisaged that vocational courses would ordinarily be provided at the higher secondary (+2) stage but flexibility was provided to start vocational education after class VIII. The NPE, 1986 set a target to cover 10 per cent of higher secondary students under vocational courses by 1990 and 25 per cent by 1995. A substantially funded centrally sponsored scheme for vocationalisation of secondary education was started with effect from February 1988. The scheme was taken for implementation in all States and Union Territories excepting Tripura, Daman and Diu, Dadra & Nagar Haveli and Lakshadweep. At the end of 1991-92, 12,543 vocational sections were approved in 4400 schools, thereby creating facilities for diversion of about 6.27 lakh students at the +2 stage (@25 students per vocational section in classes XI and XII). This accounts for 9.3 per cent of students enrolled at the +2 stage. Although quantitatively the implementation of the vocational education scheme at the +2 stage has been fairly substantial, in qualitative terms, there remains much to be done. Vocationalisation of education is identified as a priority area in the Eighth Five Year Plan.

The NPE, 1986 had also mentioned the need for non-formal and need-based vocational programmes mainly, though not exclusively, for disadvantaged groups. The NPE, 1986 also envisaged vocational courses at the tertiary level for facilitating vertical mobility. While some beginning has been made in these areas, they will receive impetus during the Eighth Plan.

The Revised Policy Formulations retain the policy framework laid by the NPE, 1986 but for two modifications. First, the target for coverage under vocational courses has been revised ten per cent of the higher secondary students by 1995 and 25 per cent by 2000. Secondly, they envisage children at the higher secondary level being imparted generic vocational courses which cut across several occupational fields and which are not occupation specific.

The vocational programme is being revised with particular emphasis on the following aspects :

— The credibility of the programme should be established. This would depend on its quality, relevance and acceptability.

— Education-employment linkages should be firmly established.

— Adequate infrastructure physical and academic should be provided.

— Assured supply of funds over an extended period of 5 to 10 years.

— Training programme for teachers both pre-service and inservice.

— Training of teacher trainers.

— Effective management structures at all levels at the Centre and in the States and reasonable tenure for their functionaries.

— Equivalence among the vocational, technical and academic courses.

— Curriculum development in consultation with employers.

— Enlisting community involvement and participation of commercial establishments and industrial houses.

— Need for active co-operation of other government departments with the Department of Education at the Central and State level.

Higher Education

India today has one of the largest systems of higher education comprising over 190 Universities and 7,000 colleges having an enrolment of over 4.4 million students with a 263 thousand strong faculty.

Several important schemes have been introduced in the last few years to restore the integrity, discipline and credibility of the system and to elevate the standards of higher education in the country. The all-India screening test for recruitment of teachers introduced in December, 1989 continues. A code of ethics and procedure for assessment and evaluation of teachers has been evolved. The system of Academic Staff Colleges for reorientation and refresher courses for teachers has been introduced. A beginning has been made for granting autonomy to selected colleges and university departments. Academic calendar has been prepared and would be continuously monitored. Andhra Pradesh has set tip a State Council of Higher Education and other States are considering setting up State Councils to coordinate development and growth of higher education in the States. Common research facilities of international standards in the fields of Nuclear Science, Astronomy, Astrophysics and Atomic Energy have been set up to provide research facilities and services. Model curricula for all disciplines have been prepared by expert committees and circulated to universities for adoption. Special assistance is being given for starting courses in emerging areas like Bio-technology, Aunospheric Science, Oceanography, Electronics and

Computer Science. Finally alternate models of university management are also being considered.

Keeping in view the needs of the system of higher education in the country the thrust areas for development identified for the future, especially during the Eighth Plan period (1992-97) are :

— Consolidation and strengthening of facilities in universities and colleges;

— Re-designing and restructuring of courses to meet the developmental needs of the country;

— Support to establishment of autonomous colleges, university departments and examination reforms, strengthening of research facilities with special reference to creation of common facilities;

— Greater involvement of students in extension activities like adult education and population education;

— Teachers' training;

— Modernisation and restructuring from within the system;

— Generation of financial resources from within the system;

— Additional enrolment of one million students in Open Universities and Distance Education System.

The Indira Gandhi National Open University (IGNOU) which was established by an Act of Parliament in September, 1985 for the introduction and promotion of the Open University and distance education systems in the educational pattern of the country and for the coordination and determination of standards in such systems, has emerged as a strong alternative at the level of higher education. The IGNOU has adopted an integrated multi-media instructional approach consisting of printed material, audio and video cassettes and counselling sessions organised during the week-end.

In pursuance of its role as national apex body for promotion, coordination and determination of standards in distance education, IGNOU has set up a Distance Education Council (DEC) as a statutory authority of the University. The DEC is initiating steps for the establishment of a network of open universities and other distance education institutions in the country.

Technical and Management Education

Technical education, which in our context also includes management education, is one of the most crucial components of human resource development with great potential for adding value to products and services and for improving the quality of life of the people. As a result of the efforts made during the successive Five Year Plans in the past on the development of technical education, the expansion of technical education in the country has been phenomenal during the past four decades.

There are,at present,over 200 recognised technical education institutions at the first degree level and more than 500 at the diploma level with the annual admission capacities of 40,000 and 80,000 students respectively. Facilities for Masters and Doctoral programmes in engineering and technology have also been created in 140 institutions with an intake of about 10,000 students per year. Five Indian Institutes of Technology (IITs) established at Bombay, Delhi, Kanpur, Kharagpur and Madras have emerged as premier centres of technical education in India. The sixth IIT is in the process of being established at Guwahati in Assam.

Specialised institutions like National Institute for Training in Industrial Engineering, National Institute of Foundry and Forge Technology, School of Planning and

Architecture, Indian School of Mines, Technical Teachers' Training Institutes and premier technical universities like University of Roorkee, Anna University, Birla Institute of Technology (Pilani), Indian Institute of Science, Bangalore and Banaras Hindu University (Institute of Technology) are important centres of technical education. In the area of management education, Indian Institutes of Management have been set up at Ahmedabad, Calcutta, Bangalore and Lucknow. Besides, there are more than 350 degree institutions and 800 diploma institutions at the State level. The National Technical Man-power Information System has been set up by the Government of India to monitor the supply and utilisation of engineering and technical man-power in the country so as to ensure a well planned development of technical education.

Some professional bodies in the fields of engineering, technology and management conduct formal and non-formal education/training programmes for fresh students as well as the working professionals and also contribute to professional development in their respective areas of activities.

The NPE, 1986 underlined the need for reorganising the technical and management education system to effectively deal with the changes in the economy, social environment, production and management processes and rapid expansion of knowledge and advances in science & technology. The NPE, 1986 laid specific guidelines for the qualitative and quantitative development of the technical and management education sectors; establishment of linkages amongst the concerned agencies; manpower assessment and technical education forecasting; increasing effectiveness of technical education management system; proper delivery systems; measures to achieve greater cost effectiveness and generation of resources through suitable means.

The various initiatives taken after the NPE include :

(i) *AICTE* : As one of the most significant achievements in the sector of technical education, the All India Council of Technical Education (AICTE) was conferred statutory status under the AICTE Act in 1987. The Council has started functioning with an independent secretariat through the various Boards of Studies and the Regional Committees. There is, however, an urgent need to strengthen the AICTE in terms of its professional and administrative functions through a process of decentralisation.

(ii) *Scheme of Continuing Education* : The scheme was started through the Indian Society for Technical Education for upgrading the skills of working professionals under which more than 200 course modules were produced which provided training to about 10,000 working professionals.

(iii) *Industry Institute Inter-action and Entrepreneurship and Management Development Programmes* : A scheme of industry-institute inter-action for forging effective and closer inter-action between technical institutions and the industry was launched. This also included establishment of an industrial foundation at IIT, Delhi and technological transfer and innovation. A scheme of entrepreneurship development for catering to the developmental needs of the non-corporate and unorganised sectors was also launched through the technical institutions.

(iv) *Curriculum Development* : A scheme for restructuring the curriculum development centres was launched for effecting curriculum development on the basis of realistic needs of the industry and the users.

(v) *Strengthening the scheme of Modernisation and Removal of Obsolescence and Thrust Areas of Technical Education* : Greater emphasis was given for covering more institutions by modernising their laboratories, workshops and teaching processes and by adopting new emerging areas of engineering and technology. This, however, needs massive financial in-puts and a strong monitoring and evaluation system as compared to the one that exists.

(vi) *World Bank Assisted Projects for Development of Technician Education :* A massive project with the assistance of World Bank was launched to enable the State Governments to upgrade their polytechnics in capacity, quality and efficiency with the total cost of Rs. 1650 crore to be implemented in two phases (1992-98) with a target of covering 500 approved polytechnics in 16 States and one Union Territory.

(vii) *Review of IIMs and TTTIs :* The IIMs and the TTTIs were reviewed by two separate National Review Committees in order to assess the present status and impact so as to give them a new thrust and direction.

(viii) *Review of Community Polytechnics:* The Scheme of Community Polytechnics was reviewed by a National Expert Committee in terms of its impact, coverage and effectiveness on the socioeconomic upliftment and poverty alleviation. The number of Community Polytechnics was also substantially increased.

(ix) *Apprenticeship Training :* In order to provide training for the 10+2 vocational students under the amended Apprentices Act, additional vocational subjects were included under the purview of the Act.

Open Education

The open learning system augments opportunities for education, ensures access, is costeffective and promotes a relevant, flexible and innovative system of education. The initial experience of the Indira Gandhi National Open University (IGNOU) and the State Open Universities, as well as the National Open School underlines the tremendous potential of the open learning system.

The IGNO which launched its academic programmes in 1987 has made significant progress. The University presently offers Bachelor's degree programmes in thirteen disciplines, a Master's degree in Business Administration, and several diploma and certificate programmes. The annual enrolment has increased from about 4,400 in 1987 to over 62,000 in 1992. The three State Open Universities, namely, Dr. B.R. Ambedkar Open University in Andhra Pradesh (BRAOU), the Kota Open University (KOU) and the Yashwantrao Chavan Maharashtra Open University in Maharashtra (YCMOU) together admitted about 65,000 students in 1992. The distance education institutions (open universities and institutes of correspondence education of conventional universities) accounted for about 11.5 per cent of the enrolment in higher education in 1990-91.

Several new programmes in employmentrelated areas are being developed by the IGNOU. Advanced Diploma programmes in Construction Management, Advanced Diploma in Irrigation and Water Resources, Postgraduate Diploma in Journalism and Mass-Communication, Bachelor's Degree in Nursing and Master's Degree in Distance Education and Library and Information Science are some of the new programmes under development by the IGNOU. The State Open Universities have also launched a number of relevant programmes in Electronics, Horticulture, Education and Communication besides the diploma and degree programmes in Humanities, Commerce and Social Sciences. The Directorates of Correspondence Education of the conventional universities have also been diversifying their programmes. These institutions are presently offering a large number of diploma and certificate programmes in technical/professional areas.

The IGNOU has set up a Distance Education Council as a statutory body for the promotion, coordination and determination of standards of the open university/ distance education system.

— The Distance Education Council will take steps for networking the State Open Universities and other distance education institutions, for sharing courses and programmes, and developing a pattern and structure for the open university programmes that would facilitate student mobility among programmes as well as institutions.

— The open university/distance education programmes would be structured on a modular pattern with provision for transfer of credits. Students will have the facility of registering for courses of their choice which, in appropriate combinations, will enable them to obtain certificates, diplomas or degrees.

— The Distance Education Council will encourage joint development of programmes and courses by IGNOU, State Open Universities and the Directorates of Correspondence

Education of conventional universities.

— It will also recommend financial assistance from IGNOU to state open universities for their development and for undertaking specific projects.

— It will initiate steps to organise programmes of training for the development of human resources for the open university/distance education system especially in such areas as course development and production, organisation of support services, etc. The possibility of establishing institutional mechanisms for this purpose will be explored.

The Distance Education Council will ultimately assume the responsibility for developing the existing correspondence education programmes on a selective basis and converting them into distance education programmes of an acceptable quality. However, for the time being, the responsibility for the development of distance education programmes in the conventional universities will remain with the UGC. There would be close consultation between the UGC and the IGNOU in the development of such programmes.

Electronic media will be progressively involved in the expansion of open learning. Doordarshan (Television) is already telecasting programmes of the IGNOU three days a week for 30 minutes from 6.30 to 7.00 a.m. The All India Radio (AIR) stations of Hyderabad and Bombay are broadcasting selected IGNOU programmes. The Hyderabad station of All India Radio has set up a transmission network in Andhra Pradesh for broadcasting the programmes offered by the BRAOU. A few of the institutes of correspondence education have made arrangements with the All India Radio for broadcasting their lessons. Distance education requires as a matter of prerequisite multimedia instruction and its success will substantially depend on the availability of facilities for broadcasting and telecasting. Efforts will be made during the Eighth Plan period to augment and network these facilities so that these programmes can reach a larger number of students.

Measures will be taken to promote the mobility of students among open universities and among the traditional universities and open universities. A significant development in this regard is the signing of the Memorandum of Understanding between the University of Pondicherry and the IGNOU which provides for recognition of each other's degrees and diplomas as well as transfer of credits for courses successfully completed by students between the two universities. Efforts will be made to promote similar arrangements with other universities.

The National Open School (NOS) already established, will be strengthened and developed to widen access to education at the secondary and higher secondary levels. Efforts will be made to establish open schools in different States so that secondary education is significantly expanded through different regional languages.

The possibility of launching vocational education programmes through the open learning system will be explored. For this purpose, meaningful linkages will be established with workstations, industries and other organisations. Such bilateral initiatives will help administer the theoretical and practical components of the vocational education packages.

The possibility of setting up a national consortium on open schooling will be explored in order to initiate coordinated steps in such areas as policy issues, priorities, long-term national and state needs, establishment of resource centres for development of materials, development of human resources for the open learning system, monitoring and evaluation of its performance, etc.

The open learning system at the secondary and tertiary levels will focus attention on education and training in areas related to employment and self-employment. It will seek the involvement of the existing institutions and organisations in commerce, industry, the service sectors as well as rural development organisations, including the mobilisation of the material and human resources in such organisations in the development of appropriate programmes and their delivery. Efforts will be made to develop close cooperation and collaboration between open education institutions and the agencies which use trained manpower both in the public and the private sectors as well as the professional organisations in various fields.

The open learning system will take steps to meet the continuing education needs of the manpower already employed in different sectors. It will help develop programmes in close cooperation with the concerned employing organisations; for training and retraining of man-power, for the upgradation of skills for application of new technologies and also in providing opportunities to serving personnel to improve their qualifications for their professional advancement. The open learning system will seek the support and cooperation of a wide spectrum of employers in the fulfilment of these objectives.

Teacher Education

A Centrally sponsored scheme of Restructuring and Reorganisation of Teacher Education is being implemented since 1987-88. It aims at Strengthening the teacher education system in the country so as to provide effective training and academic support to schools and adult and non-formal education systems.

The centrally sponsored scheme of teacher education has the following main components.

— Mass Orientation of about five lakh School Teachers (MOST) annually till 1989-90 to familiarise them with the major thrusts envisaged in the NPE and LO improve their professional competence.

— Setting-up of about 400 District Institutes of Education and Training (DIETs) either by upgrading suitable existing Elementary Teacher Education Institutions or, where necessary, by establishing new ones so as to provide total academic and training support to the elementary and adult education systems at the district level :

— Strengthening of about 250 Secondary Teacher Education Institutions (STEIs), development of about 50 of them as Institutions of Advanced Study in Education (IASEs) and the rest as Colleges; of Teacher Education (CTEs);

— Strengthening of SCERTs; and

— Establishment and strengthening of Departments of Education in Universities by the UGC.

Setting up DIETs, CTEs and IASEs is a long-gestation activity. Yet, about 150 DIETs have become operational and have started conducting training programmes. Appraisal of few such institutions sanctioned during 1987-88 is being undertaken through external agencies.

A National Council of Teacher Education was set up in 1973 to maintain standards of teacher education. The Council is being conferred statutory powers to enable it to discharge its responsibilities more effectively, including through accreditation of teacher training institutions.

Environmental Education

The concern for environmental education stems from the global concern for environment (preservation) in view of the latest developments which are emerging as a threat to the survival of the mankind. The NPE, 1986 duly accepted the importance while stating that problem of environment is a value which along with other core values, should form an integral part of the curriculum at all stages of education.The environmental education programmes thus aims at developing environmental consciousness among teachers and taught by providing knowledge base about environmental concerns through school curriculum. It also supplements the theoretical base with area specific environmental programmes so that concern for environment is well appreciated.

Government of India, started a centrally sponsored scheme of environmental orientation to school education in 1988-89 with a view to promoting integration of educational programmes in the schools with local environmental conditions. The scheme provides 100 per cent assistance to the States and voluntary agencies for taking up the various programmes/activities aimed at creating environmental consciousness among the students on project basis. It stipulates that each project area should consist of a few blocks/districts having homogeneous ecological conditions. In order to plan, co-ordinate and monitor the activities proposed to be taken up by a State, assistance is provided for creation of a State level cell. Similarly, in order to design and organise various educational programmes in schools keeping in view the local environmental conditions and concerns, assistance is provided for setting up of project cells for each project area.

The project activities include review and development of curriculum to emphasise environmental awareness; preparation of textbooks, instructional material, informative books, booklets, brochures, posters, slides, audio tapes, and films on environment; organisation of seminars for creating environmental consciousness; orientation of teachers; adoption of monuments for their up keep and maintenance study of ecological problems; etc. One of the preferred activities under the project is setting up of school nurseries. Voluntary organisations are assisted for taking up various kinds of experimental and innovative programmes in the field of environmental orientation to school education. Upto the end of March, 1992 the scheme has covered about 20,000 schools.

Although environmental education activities are concentrated at secondary level, efforts are being made to promote this component at elementary level by involving NonGovernmental Organisations (NGOs) through area specific projects. The UNESCO has also been providing assistance to NGOs in this regard. These efforts are important because, for a sustainable development, preservation and conservation of fragile and critical ecosystem is of crucial significance.

Education and Women's Empowerment

Education for Women's Equality is a vital component of the overall strategy of securing equity and social justice in education. The National Policy on Education, 1986 makes a strong and forthright statement on the intervening and empowering role of education. It emphasizes the provision of special support services and removal of factors which result in discrimination against women at all levels of education. The Policy and Programme of Action brings out clearly the need and will to devise institutional mechanism in order to ensure that gender sensitivity is reflected in the implementation of educational programmes across the board. Education for Women's Equality is too important to be left to the individual commitments or proclivities of persons in charge of implementing programmes. Therefore all agencies and institutions in the field of education are to be made sensitive and responsive to the gender dimension of educational inequities.

The role of female teachers in promoting girls' education particularly in rural areas has been emphasised in a motivational context. Therefore, during last few years women have got a preferential treatment in appointment of teachers particularly at elementary level. This is borne out by by Table 2.

Table 2. Number of Female Teachers

School Level	*No. of Teachers*	
	1986	*1990*
Higher Secondary (10+2)	125,502	144,227
	(453,538)	(466,176)
Higher Secondary (IX-XI)	6,745	NA
		(28,332)
High Schools	237,669	271,276
	(716,997)	(806,326)
Middle Schools	313,863	352,812
	(979,073)	(1,059,295)
Primary Schools	416,584	470,414
	(1,522,108)	(1,636,898)

Some of the special efforts made to promote education of girls are indicated below:

— Under the Scheme of Operation Blackboard, Government of India has provided assistance for creation of 93,303 posts of primary school teachers mainly to be filled by women. According to the latest reports, 69,926 posts of teachers have been filled up of which 57.39 percent are women teachers.

— Ninety per cent assistance was given for NFE Centres meant for girls. The cumulative number of NFE Centres for girls is 81,282.

— The Mahila Samakhya (Education for Women's Equality) Project is under implementation in the States of Gujarat, Karnataka and Uttar Pradesh with the main objective of motivating women to participate in education and providing non-formal, adult and vocational education.

— By conscious action, admission of girls to the extent of 28 per cent in Navodaya Vidyalayas has been ensured.

— Special attention was given to enrolment of women in Adult Education Centres. Under the Rural Functional Literacy Programmes. Out of 1,677 thousand adult illiterates enrolled, 914 thousand persons were women (54.50 per cent).

At the level of higher education, both general and technical, there has been a phenomenal expansion of educational opportunities for women. The response of women to avail these growing opportunities has been overwhelming as reflected by the trend in women's enrolment in all faculties and at all levels of education. Women's education at the university and college levels has been diversified and reoriented in tune with the changing requirements of society, industry and trade. More and more women have been competing for admission to specialist and professional courses year after year.

Women's enrolment in higher education institutions has grown from a mere 0.04 million in 1950-51 to 14.37 million in 1990-91, recording an increase of more than 36 times over the 40 year period. The number of women enrolled, per 100 men enrolled, during this period has gone up more than 3 times from 14 in 1950-51 to 48 in 1990-91. The enrolment of women as percentage of total enrolment has increased progressively from 27.7 per cent in 1981-82 to 29.6 percent in 1985-86 and to 32.5 per cent in 1990-91. The number of colleges meant exclusively for women has also gone up from 644 in 1981-82 to 874 in 1990-91 recording an increase of over 35 percent during the decade.

The University Grants Commission is assisting universities in promoting Women's studies to undertake research projects, development of curricula, training and extension as a motivator for various adult education programmes and as a critical instrument for social and academic development.

4

Content and Curriculum

The process of change in content of education and curriculum which was initiated as a aftermath of NPE, 1986 has made a significant impact on the teaching-learning process. The broad developments in this sphere has been on following lines:

— enrichment of curricula by cultural content;

— significant place to value education;

— use of media mid educational technology;

— integration of work experience in learning process;

— promotion of environmental consciousness;

— gearing science and mathematics teaching for promoting spirit of enquiry.

The 10+2+3 pattern of education introduced in the country envisages a broad based general education in respect of all pupils during the first ten years of school education. The curriculum at this stage is, therefore, undifferentiated and all the curricular areas are compulsory and no attempt is made to introduce diversified courses at this stage. The focus of the curriculum at the primary stage is on development of basic skills of literacy and numerary, study of environment in terms of physical and social phenomena, participation in activities which would develop productive skills, creative expression and habits of healthy living. In the initial years, the content and methodology are directed to achievement of excellence in communication and computational skills with a view to developing the basic tools of learning.

The content and process of education at the upper primary stage are directed to the consolidation of knowledge, skills, attitudes and values acquired at the lower primary stage and acquisition of wider knowledge base in the context of a broad-based general education. At this stage, the pupil is required to continue with the curricular areas introduced at the primary stage but in greater depth in terms of content and processes.

The curriculum at the secondary stage is designed to equip the children either to take up higher level courses of study to prepare for entrance into the first degree in a college or to equip them for vocational instruction at the higher secondary stage or. to enter the work force. Since secondary education continues to be terminal for a large majority of children who are likely to enter the world of work, the emphasis is on bringing their education to a standard .which would enable them to enter life with self-confidence along with useful knowledge and skills, proper work habits, attitudes and character which would contribute to their productivity and wellbeing.

There is a renewed emphasis on use of new technologies for improving education in schools. It has been envisaged that modem educational technology should reach out to the most distant areas and deprived sections of beneficiaries simultaneously with areas of comparative affluence and easy availability. Some of these programmes being implemented are described in the following paragraphs.

EDUCATIONAL TECHNOLOGY PROGRAMME

An Educational Technology Programme was started in the Central sector in the year 1972 during the Fourth Plan Period for widening access to and bringing about qualitative improvement in education. Under the scheme, a Centre for Educational Technology was set up in the NCERT and 100 per cent assistance was provided to twenty-one States for setting up Educational Technology (ET) Cells.

In view of expansion of broadcasting facilities with the advent of INSAT and concomitant demand for educational software, the Department of Education decided to take on the responsibility of production of educational television programmes for relay through satellites. Accordingly, a scheme was prepared by the Department for creating Educational Television (ETV) programme production facilities within the education sector on a decentralised basis by setting up a Central Institute of Educational Technology (CIET) in the NCERT and State Institutes of Educational Technology (SIETs) in six States, viz., Andhra Pradesh, Bihar, Gujarat, Maharashtra, Orissa and Uttar Pradesh and strengthening of ET Cells in other States.

The Educational Technology Scheme was revised in 1987 with the broad objectives of strengthening of both ETV and audio programme production capabilities and providing wider access to the same by supplying one lakh Colour Television (CTV) sets and five lakh Radio-Cum-Cassette Players (RCCPs) to primary schools during the Seventh Plan.

Programme production has commenced in CIET and all the six SIETs. In fact, from the academic year 1988-89, responsibility for programme production, which was until then being shared between CIET and Doordarshan on 50:50 basis, has been taken over by CIET and SIETs.

The satellite based ETV service presently provides telecast of educational programmes for the children and their teachers at the primary level in the morning for 45 minutes duration in each of the five regional languages, namely Gujarati, Hindi, Marathi, Oriya mid Telugu on time sharing basis. The programmes for children are telecast from Monday to Friday and for primary level teachers on every Saturday. There are separate programmes for the children in the age groups of 5-8 and 9-11 years on each day.

The ETV programmes are relayed by all high and low power transmitters in the six INSAT States. The programmes in Hindi are relayed in the States of Haryana, Himachal Pradesh, Madhya Pradesh, Punjab and Rajasthan and the Union Territory of Chandigarh.

An ambitious programme of distribution of CTV sets and RCCPs was undertaken under the ET Scheme. Funds are also being sanctioned for audio programme production by State Governments and non-Government organisations. The CIET has also produced more than 1100 audio programmes on various educational themes at various levels of school education. SIETs have also geared efforts towards production of audio programmes either by themselves and/or through outside agencies. A list of about 40 video and audio programmes produced by the CIET have been identified for providing meaningful media support to the DIETs in their teacher training activities.

Computer Education in Schools

A pilot project on Computer Literacy and Studies in Schools (CLASS) was initiated in 1984-85 in 248 selected secondary/higher secondary schools jointly by the Department of Electronics and the Department of Education to acquaint students and teachers with the range of computer applications and its potential as a learning medium. Till 1989-90, 2,598 schools were covered under the project. Sixty-one resource centres were set up to train school teachers and provide logistic support to the participating schools. Installation of hardware and its maintenance is the responsibility of Computer Maintenance Corporation (CMC) and the NCERT is the nodal agency for software development, academic support and organisation of teachers' training.

The Steering Committee for the project is jointly headed by the Secretaries of the Department of Electronics and the Department of Education. Upto 1986-87, the schools received a set of two BBC Micros. This number was increased to five BBC Micros from 1987-88 on-wards. Since the last financial year, a decision has been taken to provide an additional three BBC Micros to those old schools (1249) which have so far only two computers each. Therefore, no new schools have been added since 1990-91. The project is currently under review for streamlining its implementation.

Higher Education

The University Grants Commission introduced the scheme of restructuring of courses with a view to making the first degree courses more relevant to environment and to the developmental needs of the community and to link education with work/field/practical experience and productivity.

The scheme has been conceived as a major programme for reforms in higher education at the undergraduate level. The programme aims at imparting training to every undergraduate student in the following areas:

i) A set of foundation courses designed to create an awareness of areas such as Indian History and

Culture, History of the Freedom Struggle in India and other part of the world, Social and Economic Life in India including concepts and processes of development, scientific methods including the role of science and technology in development, alternative value systems and societies based thereon, Cultures of Asia and Africa and Gandhian thought.

ii) A set of core courses to give an opportunity to students to acquire broad familiarity with some chosen disciplines, including study of one or more of them in depth.

iii) Some applied studies/projects/field activity to form an integral activity of the course and to be carried out in the final year.

iv) Involvement in a programme of national or social service for the first two years.

Nine universities and 208 colleges have introduced restructured courses under the scheme upto March 1991. The Commission has also desired that the work of restructuring of courses may be undertaken on the pattern of Curriculum Development Centres.

Some of the important programmes launched to improve teaching-learning process include:

— College Humanities and Social Science Improvement Programme (COHSSIP)
— College Science Improvement Programme (COSIP)
— University Leadership Programmes
— Special Assistance Programmes (SAP)
— Curriculum Development Centres

Mass Communication and Educational Technology

(a) Country-wide classroom programmes

The University Grants Commission has been allocated

two hours transmission time daily for six days a week for telecasting 'Country-wide Class-room' programmes relating to higher education. The programmes are essentially enrichment programmes meant to take education to remote, rural and backward areas of the country.

(b) Race to save the planet

The University Grants Commission, which was involved in collaboration with a premier public broadcasting Corporation, WGBH, Boston in producing a ten-part television series entitled 'Race to Save the Planet' is telecasting the series on Doordarshan network from 14th October, 1990 on Sundays. The programmes of the series have been shot all over the world including the Antarctica. The series analyses and presents the most important dilemma of our times, viz., how to reconcile the urge of growth and development with the need to preserve and improve the environment and enhance the quality of human living. The series also comes at a time when awareness of these problems is on the increase, both within the country and abroad. It also lends perspective to the story of the human happening on the planet and provides some wisdom to choose the specificities of our development agenda.

Educational Research

A large number of institutions across the country are involved in promotion and conduct of educational research in India. During the last 40 years, more than 4,000 research studies in the area of education have been completed. The bulk of these studies have been carried out at university departments and a majority of them are doctoral research studies. These doctoral studies are conducted by research scholars who receive fellowships for this purpose from University Grants Commission, the Indian Council for Social Science Research and such other national bodies in order to ensure the competence and aptitude of the scholars for doing research, the University Grants Commission has been conducting a specially designed eligibility test at the national level for receiving Research Fellowships.

A major limitation of doctoral research work is that these studies have a relatively narrower conception and applicability as they are carried out by individual scholars working under constraints of time as well as resources. In order to overcome these constraints there has been a greater thrust during the recent years, to carry out research projects at institutional level with a long-term perspective and commitment. Towards this end, the national funding agencies have been specifying priority areas for promoting research so that the findings of die research can be effectively utilised for planning and policy making.

The University Grants Commission promotes educational research by providing funds for the purpose to universities and colleges. The Commission has been operating various schemes such as Centres of Advanced Studies, Departments of Special Assistance and Departmental Research Support. Under these schemes selected university departments which have capabilities in terms of qualified manpower are encouraged to pursue research vigorously and for this purpose necessary support is extended by way of providing equipment, consumable items, contingent expenditure, etc. The Commission also continues to support university/college teachers for undertaking research through such schemes as Minor Research Project, Major Research Project, Career Award and Research Scientist Schemes. In order to cater to the information needs of the researchers, the Commission has established National Information

Centres in Science, Humanities and Social Sciences including Education. In fact programmes of strengthening them have received very high priority.

National Council of Educational Research and Training, promotes research on different aspects of school education through in house research projects as well as through funding of research studies taken up by outside individuals and institutions. The research activities of the Council are monitored by a specially constituted committee called "Educational Research and Innovations Committee" (ERIC). The ERIC helps to identify priority areas in research and sanctions funds for research projects undertaken by the departments of the NCERT. Currently, the ERIC is encouraging national level researches in three priority areas, namely, universalisation of elementary education, vocationalisation of education and curriculum development.

The National Institute of Educational Planning and Administration also has been carrying out research studies in the field of educational planning and administration. Till recently, the research activities of the Institute were limited to in-house projects carried out by its faculty members. However, during 1987-88, the Institute initiated a research grant scheme for promoting research on various aspects of educational planning and administration by outside individuals and institutions.

Education for Cultural Development

With more than 4000 communities, 18 constitutionally recognised languages and hundreds of dialects, more than six major religious and hundreds of sects and more than 800 million people, India presents a very complex, plural culture which very nearly permeates every aspect of living from patterns of belief and values to hundreds of forms of creative articulation, from costumes mid foods to enormous subtleties of refinement and participation. Nothing in India can possibly escape the impact of its culture, be it politics, technology, education or development. Even the long colonial subjugation had a distinctively Indian hue while it shared many aspects with similar colonised countries.

The strong and inescapable cultural implications of education and development were recognised right from the beginning of the epic scale national reconstruction which was launched when the recently free India gave to itself, in the early fifties, a new constitution and the form of a democratic republic. In many ways India's democratic ethos and its amazing survival owes as much to the political sagacity of its people as to their innate sense of culture, their unfailing cultural literacy inspite of their depressing poverty mid widespread verbal literacy. It is the age-old resilience of Indian traditions that made them show genuine openness to new ideas while remaining firmly rooted and have, therefore, evolved their own distinctive dynamics of change and absorption.The built in resistance in Indian milieu to tyranny of any kind, whether of belief or truth or behaviour, has made it face new challenges with confidence and bring about many transmutations without tensions of rupture. The issue of education, culture and development have to be seen in this context of an enriching, if also a trifle perplexing, continuum.

Each linguistic and racial group has its own distinct cultural identity. Yet interaction has taken and continues to take place amongst regions, between different an disciplines at various levels of society, from the most affluent to the weakest sections. Culture has always been an integral part of the informal process of an Indian's education, contributing to the integrated development of his personality, sensitising him towards his environment and his natural and cultural heritage. In the present day scenario, when the world is facing numerous problems such as dissension and intolerance, destruction of the natural environment, wars and poverty, the role of culture in the developmental effort, and particularly in education, cannot be over-emphasised. It is now widely recognised that only the integration of our artistic and cultural with curriculum teaching will make the young aware of the aesthetic dimensions of life and senstitise them towards creative expression.

Education plays a very important culturising role. The converse is equally true: Culture plays a very important educating role. Both the National Policy on Education, 1986 and the Approach to the National Policy on Culture (NPC) constantly emphasise the cultural consequences of education and seek to strengthen its cultural components. As stated in the NPE 1986, "deculturalisation, dehumanisation and alienation must be avoided at all costs. Education can mid must bring about a fine synthesis between change oriented technologies and the country's continuity of cultural tradition. The curricula and processes of education will be enriched by cultural content in a many manifestations as possible. Children will be enabled to develop sensitivity to beauty, harmony and refinement". The Approach to the NPC also commits itself to the growth of cultural literacy along with verbal literacy and inculcation of respect and striving for creativity and excellence from the earliest levels of education.

School Curricula and the Role of Education in Cultural Development

The inter-linking of education and culture seeks to discover the inherent talent and potential of a child and develop his personality. With this in view, a Programme of Action has been formulaed under the NPE, right from the pre-primary stage to the highest level of formal education. Some of the salient features of this culture-education linkage are mutual participation, use of inexpensive and relevant material for cultural exposure, promotion of a concept of cultural neighborhood involving active participation of the community, curriculum reform motivation and training of teachers, and efforts to encourage the young to participate in cultural activities. The cultural input in school education seeks to sensitise the child towards his environment and natural materials around him, and teach him to appreciate the aesthetic forms and rhythms he grows up with. The school child is also provided a basic core of facts about India's cultural heritage through folk songs, local history and archaeological artefacts. A sense of design and aesthetics is encouraged. Teacher training programmes also seek to enhance their capability for cultural instruction. Special books, educational material and audio visual facilities are also sought to be provided for schools.

Resource persons in the community, irrespective of their formal educational qualification are being invited to contribute to the cultural enrichment of education employing both the literate and oral traditions. To sustain and carry forward the cultural tradition, the role of old masters, who trained pupils through traditional modes is being supported and recognised. India is striving to promote a symbiosis between local environment, indigenous technologies, oral traditions of literature and the demands of keeping pace with the rapid technological advances.

The languages of India have been very valuable vehicles of cultural articulation and dissemination. Development of linguistic skills and a sense of pride in mother tongues is sought to be encouraged at all levels. Learning of our classical languages and training in traditional disciplines available only in them are being seen as preservation of an important aspect of our cultural heritage and its continuing relevance.

Interaction between the Schools, the Community and the Society

The NPE as well as the approach to the NPC seek to encourage educational institutions to be in live contact with local writers. artists etc. as cultural education should be seen not as an additional burden on but as an integrated component in curriculum teaching. School Community interaction is sought to be institutionalised by getting local artisans, craftsmen etc. to teach/ demonstrate their art to school-children.

Organisation of regular visits to monuments, museums and sanctuaries is also being encouraged. Development of conservation ideas through adoption of monuments by the students and the community, taking their help to keep the monuments clean and safeguarding them will make the youth aware of their natural as well as man-made environment.

Apart from setting up small museum comers in schools, the established museums are being encouraged to reorient themselves as active centres for awareness building regarding cultural heritage. Museums have to function as more than storehouses of our ancient heritage. They have a vital role as centres of learning and education. Museum visits are sought to be systematically encouraged with each Museum developing attractive programmes which would interest the young.

One of the major thrusts of the NPC would be the expansion of library facilities in the rural areas. The rural library movement is sought to be intensified through the setting up of a network of rural libraries linked with the District Library System. This would take care of the reading needs of the student community and the growing numbers of educated youth.

Training of Teachers for a New Responsibility

India started inservice training programmes two decades ago in the area of linking education with culture. The Centre for Cultural Resources and Training (CCRT) was set up at the nationol level to provide a cultural component in curriculum teaching and a number of teachers and teacher-educators trained in this institution are doing commendable work in schools and State Institutes of Education. CCRT training programmes are designed to enable teachers to acquire knowledge of the use of the arts and crafts in the service of education, to create an awareness of India's cultural heritage, and to inculcate a sense of appreciation of the multiple levels of cultural interaction in the country. CCRT also strives to sensitise the decision makers on the need for cultural education, especially to appreciate the role of the youth in the preservation of the natural and cultural heritage.

The content of the teacher training covers different aspects of India's heritage the environment and geography, the historical evolution of traditions. art and culture architecture, sculpture, music. dance forms, theatre, with emphasis on regional forms and handicrafts. In order to make teacher training adaptable for practical use in the classroom, it incorporates lesson plans integrating aspects of culture with curriculum work, preparation of innovative educational aids directly involving the child in the learning process, and demonstration of new methodologies. Practical classes in music, movement and mime, traditional crafts and technical skills are arranged to help teachers to discover the child's potential and talent and create a balance between academic studies and practical work. A Cultural kit which includes slides and recorded cassettes as well as books and explanatory notes is provided to the schools from which teachers have been trained. Educational tours to places of historical and cultural interest, museums and aft galleries are organised. The first-hand experience helps teachers understand how such visits can complement classroom teaching. Since its inception, the CCRT has trained 26,710 teachers/principals/district education officers. Besides, 33;388 students have also been directly trained by the Centre.

Each district in India is to set up a District Institute of Education and Training for training teachers at the primary level. The syllabus of this training highlights the need for an understanding of the local cultures. In some of these DIETs, resource persons trained by the CCRT are providing methodologies for a cultural input at the primary level. Colleges of teacher training are also considering a cultural input in the pre-service curriculum.

Most States in India have Centres for Educational Research and Training. Each such Centre has a special wing related to cultural education. Several voluntary agencies in the rural areas are doing admirable work in the area of education, taking into account the local culture and needs.

Internal Cooperation

India is one of the leading countries in promoting the ideal and objectives of the UNESCO. The Indian National Commission for Cooperation with UNESCO (INC), is the apex advisory, executive, liaison, information and the coordinating body at the national level. INC has been playing the principal role in UNESCO's work particularly in the formulation and execution of its programme in collaborating with National Commissions of Asia and Pacific region.

India continues to extend its cooperation to UNESCO workshops and its regional offices through participation in numerous symposia and conferences, organising national, regional and inter-regional activities in India in areas of competence of UNESCO, arranging placement of UNESCO fellows in Indian Institutions, implementing projects under the Participation Programme of UNESCO and administration of UNESCO Coupons scheme. Public Information activities relating to UNESCO continued to be operated in the form of publication of Hindi and Tamil editions of UNESCO Courier.

The country being one of the promoters of UNESCO's Regional Programme of Educational Innovations for Development of Asia and the Pacific (APEID), participation in APEID programmes and activities continue at a significant scale. A National Development Group (NDG) for APEID in India has been set up which functions as an identifier, stimulater and coordinator of activities of educational innovations for development within the country. The NDG, which is headed by Secretary, Department of Education, comprises representatives of concerned Ministries and Departments and pioneering institutions engaged in educational research.

On the lines of NDG, State Development Groups (SDGs) have also been established in States and Union Territories which function in, close collaboration with the NDG. The NCERT, one of the principal associate centres of APEID, acts as the secretariat of NDG and facilitates dissemination of information about APEID activities, innovative experiences at the regional level and making outcomes of the regional cooperation within APEID known widely in the country.

One of the most important regional programme of UNESCO in which India has contributed significantly is the Asia-Pacific Programme on Education for All (APPEAL) which was launched from New Delhi by UNESCO in 1987. With an overriding concern to wipe out illiteracy from the face of the earth by the year 2000, UNESCO designated 1990 as the International Literacy Year (ILY) to focus global attention on the need to initiate, promote and consolidate measures for eradication of illiteracy completely by the year 2000. The high level National Coordination Committee, set up by India to coordinate activities under APPEAL and EFA, met on September 6, 1991 tinder the Chairmanship of Education Secretary. Government of India.

The sixth meeting of the National Coordination Committee on APPEAL and EFA took ńote of the programmes launched in the fields of adult education and literacy, elementary education and universalisation of primary education. The Committee was also apprised of the components of strategy for universalisation of primary education which had emerged after an evaluative study of the projects. The Committee made a number of recommendations particularly with regard to universalisation of primary education.

The twenty-first session of the INC was held on July 22,1991 under the Chairmanship of Shri Arjun Singh, Minister of Human Resource Development. The session of the National Commission was preceded by the meetings of the Sub-Commissions on Education, Natural Sciences, Social Sciences, Culture and Communication. The principal matters which were discussed related to the Draft Programme and Budget of the UNESCO for 1992-93. The session gave detailed consideration to the recommendations made by the Sub-Commissions on the Draft Programme of UNESCO for evolving a national perspective and strategic approach to the issues which were to come up for consideration at the 26th Session of the General Conference of UNESCO. At the XXI Session,

Draft Resolutions to be moved at the General Conference were approved and guidelines were laid down on the national stand which the Indian Delegation should take on matters or issues to be raised in the 26th Session of the General Conference of UNESCO.

India participated in twenty-sixth session of the General Conference of UNESCO held at Paris from 15th October to 7th November, 1991.

The leader of the Indian delegation Shri Arjun Singh, Minister of Human Resource Development delivered a statement in Hindi in the Plenary Session on 18th October, 1991. This was for the first time that the leader of the Indian delegation addressed the General Conference in Hindi.

The Minister of Human Resource Development (HRM) in his statement highlighted the need for the entire UN system, including UNESCO, to equip itself to deal with new challenges ahead. tic said that the new era of global interdependence required the culture of multilateralism and democracy. The HRM emphasised that the 26th General Conference was grappling seriously to improve the programme delivery of UNESCO through structural refroms. He also offered India's full cooperation to the proposed International Commission on Education in the 21st Century.

External academic relations both bilateral and multilateral perform a significant role in international diplomacy. With a view to deepen India's academic interaction with important countries the educational component of the Cultural Exchange Programmes and other bilateral arrangements are being implemented vigorously. New avenues are being explored to encourage studies regarding India and Indology in Foreign Universities. Institution to Institution linkages in areas of relevance to India are being promoted. Selected Indian

Missions abroad have also been approached to take active interest in promoting bilateral collaboration in the field of education. A dialogue has been established to concretise new ideas in this area with our Missions in China, Pakistan, Japan, USA, Germany, Bhutan, France, etc.

International Literacy Prizes

UNESCO has instituted International Literacy Prizes which are awarded annually in recognition of the services of institutions, organisations or individual displaying outstanding merit and achieving special success in contributing to the fight against illiteracy. The award of the prizes is also intended to stimulate the sympathy and support of public opinion for literacy programmes in progress. On the recommendation of the INC, UNESCO has awarded Noma Literacy Prize to the Government of West Bengal for its outstanding contribution to the fight against illiteracy. The value of the Prize is $10,000/-. The prize was presented by Director General, UNESCO to the representative of the Government of West Bengal at a function in Paris on 8 September, 1991. Puduvai Arivoli Iyakkam of Pondicherry has been awarded UNESCO's 'King Sejong Literacy Prize' for the year 1992 for having meticulously planned literacy and post-literacy campaigns. The King Sejong Literacy Prize was awarded in 1990 to the Kerala Sastra Sahitya Parishad, Trivandrum.

Exchange of Scholars and Students

India also has bilateral, cultural exchange programmes, including educational programmes with more than 60 countries. The cultural exchange programme is a mutual process in which the Government of India sends delegations to other countries for studying their educational systems and innovative practices and also receives similar delegations from other countries. This part, India participates in several programmes of bilateral and multilateral import, providing for the exchange of scholars through a number of scholarship and fellowship schemes.

For the promotion of goodwill and friendly relations, 180 scholarships are offered every year by Government of India, to the nationals of selected African, Asian and other developing countries for under-graduate and post-graduate studies in India. Also, as a member of the Commonwealth, India participates in a number of programmes of exchange of scholars from among the various Commonwealth member countries. Under the Technical Cooperation Scheme of the Colombo Plan, the Government of India offers assistance for placement of scholars coming from different countries of the sub-region.

Also, more than hundred scholarships are offered every year to the nationals of Bangladesh for higher studies in India. Apart from operating these specific programmes of cooperation at the regional and sub-regional levels, India is extending active support and cooperation for educational development by offering the services of its scholars to various other countries and also by providing facilities for higher education at Indian Universities for scholars from a number of developing countries, particularly from Asian and African continents.

Joint Research

In the field of technical education some of the leading technical institutions of the country have international collaboration projects under umbrella agreements through the Department of Economic Affairs and the Department of Science and Technology of the Government of India. At present, such collaborations are with institutions in advanced countries like the USA, United Kingdom, Germany, France, Italy, Switzerland, Canada, Norway and Sweden. Besides transfer of technology, the specific objectives of such collaborations are joint research and manpower development in emerging areas of science and technology.

Book Promotion

In the area of Book Promotion, India has undertaken a number of bilateral as well as multilateral programmes. In the publication of low-priced university level books of foreign origin, the Department of Education is operating three programmes in collaboration with UK and USSR. Under this project. the latest edition of standard foreign university-level text and reference books for which comparable Indian books are not available, are taken up for publication in low-priced edition. A new import and export policy for book publication also came into force from April 1988 and will be effective until March 1991. Under this policy, recognised educational, scientific, technical and research institutions as also the Central and State Government Departments engaged in research and development work can import educational equipment as specified in their areas of specialisation.

Externally Assisted Projects on Basic Education

The reflective process which culminated in the formulation of the National Policy on Education, 1986 (NPE) and the Programme of Action highlighted two factors which inhibited the achievement of the goal of UEE resources and systemic deficiencies. The Government of India has been trying to harness the interest of bilateral and multilateral agencies in basic education an outcome of the World Conference on Education For All, held in Jomtien, Thailand, in March

1990 to take up projects which would serve as the lead and model for the systemic changes needed to realise the elusive goals.

Over the last few years there has been a qualitative change in the perceptions on primary education and adult education. A holistic view of basic education has replaced sectoral and narrow view of primary, non-formal and adult education. In this context Basic Education comprises:

a) Universalisation of Primary Education, viewed as a composite programme of (i) access to primary education for all children upto 14 years of age; (ii) universal participation till they complete the primary stage through formal or non-formal education programme; and (iii) universal achievement at least of minimum levels of learning;

b) Functional literacy, in which self reliant skills in three R's are emphasised, alongwith relevant education relating to the needs of the individual, the family and the community;

c) Special emphasis on women's education and development in order to ensure that they move towards equality in education and become the instruments and beneficiaries of the development process; and

d) Post-literacy, continuing education and inculcation of basic skills for survival and general well-being.

An access syndrome afflicts educational planning. Physical access and inputs opening of new schools, construction of school buildings and appointment of teachers are predominant concerns to the neglect of other inter-related issues which have a bearing on the ultimate outcomes. What is required is a holistic approach which, inter alia, encompasses the following:

(i) address the more difficult aspects of access,viz., setting up and operating a really good system of NFE for out of school working children and girls;

(ii) focus on the education of girls and women;

(iii) attention to issues of quality, content and process of education;

(iv) decentralised planning, community involvement and enlistment of all the 'concerned' persons and agencies such as NGOs and teachers in the formulation and implementation of the project;

(v) effective and participative management structures from the village to state level which would make the system work better, e.g., teacher attendance, timely supply of textbooks, improved retention and achievement, etc.;

(vi) development of resource institutions;

(vii) training of teachers and all other functionaries involved in the project; and

(viii) innovation testing, trial and experimentation of new models of programmes and management.

The modalities for raising external resources for basic education were discussed by the Central Advisory Board of Education (CABE) at its 46th meeting on 8-9 March, 1991. The following parameters for external funding approved by the CABE are being followed in negotiations with donor agencies and within the Government:

i) The external funding should be an additionality to the resources for education.

ii) The project must be in total conformity with the national policies, strategies and programmes.

iii) The project formulation should be the responsibility of the Centre/State Governments/other national agencies and that project formulation should be a process of capacity building.

iv) The project must be drawn up on innovative lines emphasising people's participation, improvement of quality and equality of education and a substantial upgradation of facilities.

The CABE had noted that in the implementation of the externally aided projects, the State Governments were handicapped by the stipulation requiring the States to first incur expenditure from their own resources and claim reimbursement subsequently. The CABE, therefore, recommended a specially earmarked ways and means advance to the States for the implementation of externally aided projects. At the 47th meeting of CABE on 5-6 May, 1992, the Board reiterated these recommendations of the 46th meeting and further advised that the external assistance should be used for educational reconstruction which should go beyond conventional measures such as opening new schools, appointing teachers and address issues of content, process and quality. This approach is necessarily more process oriented.

The following Projects with funding by external resources in the area of basic education are in various stages of formulation and implementation:

Under Implementation

— Andhra Pradesh Primary Education Project (APPEP) with Overseas Development Administration (UK) assistance.

— Rajasthan Project (Shiksha Karmi) with Swedish International Development Authority (SIDA) assistance.

— Mahila Samakhya (Education for Women's Equality Programme) with Dutch assistance.

— Bihar Education Project with UNICEF assistance.

— Rajasthan Lok Jumbish Project with Swedish International Development Authority (SIDA) assistance.

Under Formulation

U.P. Basic Education Project with World Bank assistance.

Under Conceptualisation

— South Orissa Project

— M.P. Basic Education Project

— M.P. Tribal Education Project

The Andhra Pradesh Primary Education Project (APPEP),Shiksha Karmi and Mahila Samakhya were formulated before the Jomtein Conference and deal with primary schooling, teacher absenteeism in remote areas and women's education respectively. After the Jomtien Conference the holistic view of Basic Education is being accepted while formulating externally assisted projects.

ODA Assisted Andhra Pradesh Primary Education Project (APPEP)

This project is being implemented in Andhra Pradesh, since April, 1983 with the assistance of Overseas Development Administration (ODA) of U.K. The objective of the project is to improve the quality of primary education in the project area by (a) providing primary school buildings and class rooms of improved quality; and (b) enhancing the professional competence of teachers and supervisors of primary schools through HRD programme.

6.8 Phase-I of the project covering 330 schools spread across 11 districts in A.P. came to an end in 1987. Phase-

II of the project spans the period 1989-90 to 1995-96 and would cover all the primary schools in A.P. The project envisages an outlay of 31.1 (in Pound) million.

Shiksha Karmi Project

The Shiksha Karmi Project in Rajasthan seeks to tackle the problem of teacher absenteeism. The crucial innovation is the substitution of the primary school teacher by a team of voluntary education workers Shiksha Karmis who would be selected by the local community and imparted intensive training. The project has a strong component of training inputs. It aims to cover in a phased manner about 1050 remote villages in 70 blocks of Rajasthan. The total outlay on the project for the period June 1991 to June 1996 is Rs. 41.23 crore. Ninety per cent of the outlay is being reimbursed by Swedish International Development Authority (SIDA).

Mahila Samakhya

Mahila Samakhya Programme (Education for Women's Equality) was launched with Dutch assistance in 10 districts of Gujarat, Karnataka and Uttar Pradesh in April 1989. The programme has been designed keeping in view the existing situation of women in the rural areas and addresses itself to the poorest women. The Mahila Samakhya Project pre-supposes that education can be a decisive intervention towards women's equality. Its overall goal is to create predicament, to move from a state of abject dis-empowerment towards a situation in which they can determine their own lives and influence their environment, and simultaneously create for themselves and their family an educational opportunity which serves the process of their development.

Over the last three years the project has had a visible impact in the villages covered. Women have been able to address themselves to problems like access to drinking water, payment of minimum wages, access to health services, ensuring 30 per cent reservation in the Jawahar Rozgar Yojana, functioning of the village school, children's participation in education, and domestic and social violence. Systematic inputs to educate rural women on their legal rights has been an important focus in the project. Hundred per cent Dutch assistance is available for the project on reimbursement basis. During the Eighth Plan period, it is proposed to cover ten additional districts in the existing three States and also to expand the scheme into Andhra Pradesh.

Lok Jumbish

The project 'Lok Jumbish: People's Movement for Basic Education for All Rajasthan' is being taken up with SIDA's assistance in Rajasthan. The Project relics heavily on people's mobilisation and seeks to bring about maximum possible decentralisation of management, accountability and relevance to the educational system. The overall goal of the project is to achieve education for all in Rajasthan by the year 2000. The expenditure is proposed to be shared among SIDA, Government of India and Government of Rajasthan in the ratio 3:2:1. It is estimated that the total project outlay over a ten year period would be approx. Rs.5000-6000 million. In the pilot phase (1992-94) 25 blocks are being covered.

Bihar Education Project

The Bihar Education Project (BEP) has been conceived as a societal mission for bringing about fundamental change in the basic education system and through it the overall socio-cultural situation. The BEP covers all components of basic education and will be expanded in a phased manner to cover 150 blocks in 20 districts.

Project activities have begun in seven districts. An outlay of Rs.3600 million is envisaged for BEP during 1990-95 of which the UNICEF will contribute Rs. 1 800 million, Government of India Rs.1200 million and Government of Bihar Rs.600 million. A simultaneous process of mobilisation and micro-planning characterises the project. The most important characteristic of the BEP management is a mission mode which pre-supposes a time bound scheme of things in which specific responsibility is attached to institutions, agencies, or individuals. Accordingly, the management of the project has been vested in a State-level autonomous registered body namely 'Bihar Shiksha Pariyojana Parishad' (BSPP) which has been constituted having two bodies a Council with the Chief Minister as Chairman, and an Executive Committee with State Education Secretary as its Chairman. Representation of teachers, NGOs, Government of India and institutions of national stature has been secured in the deliberative bodies of BSPP. The executive responsibility vests with the State Project Director

Uttar Pradesh Basic Education Project

It is proposed to formulate a test case basic education project in U.P. with World Bank assistance covering ten districts of U.P. with ten Piggy Bank districts to be treated as reserve for speedy utilisation of funds. The State Government of U.P. has prepared a project which is with the World Bank for appraisal. The draft project envisages an outlay of approx. Rs.5500 million during the period 1992-97.

South Orissa Project

Possibility is being explored to mobilise external resources for a project in the four most backward tribal districts of South Orissa. The South Orissa Project outline seeks to impart education oriented to the problems of the local environment and combines education with skill and enterpreneurship development.

'Roopantar' an Education For All Project in Madhya Pradesh and 'Dhumkuria' an Educational Project for Tribal Areas of Madhya Pradesh

Possibility is being explored to mobilise external resources for an Education for All Project in M.P. and another educational project for tribal areas of M.P. with assistance from EEC and UNESCO respectively. It is proposed that in the project 'Roopantar' the EFA project in M.P. in the first phase the four districts of Mandsaur, Sidhi, Raisen and Raigarh will be covered in full while there will be partial coverage of two districts of Satna and Dhar. The outlay for Phase I is Rs.648 million. The second phase will be spread over July 1994 to June 1999. Hundred blocks are proposed to-be covered,and the estimated outlay for this phase would be Rs.4035.3 million. The project proposal 'Dhumkuria' an educational project for tribal areas of M.P. is also under preparation with the assistance of UNESCO. Five districts are proposed to be covered over a period of three years at an estimated outlay of Rs.605.3 million.

5

Fifty Years of Educational Development

India made its tryst with destiny on 15th August 1947. Independence meant the important task of rebuilding the nation and in this, education had an important place. It convened two conferences in January 1948, within a few months from attaining Independence viz. The Conference of the Central Advisory Board of Education (CABE) and an All India Conference of Provincial Ministers of Education. At these Conferences, consideration was given to urgent educational problems confronting independent India and some important and far-reaching decisions were made including the one of attainment of compulsory basic education.

Status of Education Inherited

At the time of Independence, there were 1,40,794 Primary schools (1,26,982 for boys and 13,812 for girls), each school serving an area of approximately 5 miles; there were 12,899 middle/secondary schools (11,081 for boys and 1,818 for girls), there were 20 Universities and 591 colleges (459 Arts and Science colleges and 132 professional). The enrolment in primary schools stood at 115.38 latch (84.28 lakh boys and 31.10 lakh girls) representing 36.3% of the school-going population at the primary school stage (6 to 11 years). The literacy percentage in accordance with the census data of 1951 was 16.67% only (24.95% for male and 7.93% for female). Thus, the education system was beset with a number of problems e.g. fewer educational institutions, regional imbalance, gender disparities, absence of vocational and technical education, lack of uniform curricula and an emphasis on English education in the main.

The need for a literate population and universal education were given due recognition during the freedom struggle. Mahatma Gandhi while leading the freedom struggle against colonial rule advocated basic education and proposed an alternative village and community based system of education.

Management of Education

Constitutional Basis

In the pre-independence era, development of education was guided by the Acts, Despatches (Wood's despatch) Reports of Commissions and Committees. In the post-Independence era, the framers of the Constitution accorded due importance to education and Article 45 of the Constitution enjoined that "The State shall endeavour to provide, within a period of 10 years from the commencement of the Constitution, for free and compulsory education for all children until they complete the age of 14 years." The Constitution thus placed an obligation on the State to provide, free and compulsory education. The Constitution also enjoined educational tights fix minorities and for the educational development of weaker sections of society.

The subject of education continued to be on the State List till 1976 when, through the 42nd Amendment of the

Constitution, it was brought to the Concurrent List in the Constitution for fulfilment of nationally accepted goals. The 73rd and 74th Constitutional Amendments further contributed to educational development. Panchayati Raj Institutions were strengthened by these amendments which opened a new era for development of education at the grass roots level. In 1997, the Central Government has introduced a Fundamental Rights Bill for making elementary education into a Fundamental Right and making it obligatory for parents to educate their children in the age group 6-14 years.

Participatory Involvement

Educational development is a Participatory process. Contributions made by educational experts have been immense, given byway of recommendations of CABE and a number of other Commissions and Committees from time to time. Although a number of Commissions have made recommendations on various aspects of educational policy, mention can only be made of a few such as the Radhakrishnan Commission (1949) relating to University Education, the Mudaliar Commission (1952) relating to Secondary Education,the Kothari Commission (1964-66) which was a more comprehensive Commission suggesting reforms in all sectors of education.

Policy and Educational Developments through Five Year Plans

When in 1951, India took to the nation rebuilding process through Five Year Plans, educational development efforts were also regulated through the plan mechanism. On the basis of the Kothari Commission Report as well as the report of the Committees of the Members of Parliament, a Resolution on National Policy on Education was issued by the Government on July 24, 1968 which came to be regarded as the first National Policy on Education in free India. The National Policy Resolution called for a transformation of the system of education, to regulate it more closely to the lives of the people, called for continuous efforts to expand educational opportunities and for sustained efforts to raise the quality of education at all stages. It emphasised also on the development of science and technology, and laid stress on qualitative moral and social values. The National Policy Resolution inter-alia also gave importance to work experience, social and national services as an integral part of education at all stages. Expansion of education through part time, distance education and vocational studies were also to be a part of overall educational strategy.

Concept of Human Resource Development

In the evolution of educational policy, the year 1985 is another landmark as in that year the Ministry of Human Resource Development was set up which marked institutionalisation of the idea i.e. to build the country's human resource holistically which should be looked upon as the most valuable resource and that development should look beyond economic growth with its calculus of the Gross National Product (GNP). Emphasis was placed oil development aiming at the integrated development of citizens beginning with childhood and continuing right through life. The objective was to bring about a coordinated integrated approach ill regard to programmes affecting human resource development.

Subsequently, the government reviewed the education system and initiated a national debate on education. Based on the suggestions received, a new National Policy on Education (NPE) 1986 and its Programme of Action, 1992 were prepared in consultation with the State Governments and adopted by the Parliament.

The NPE, 1986 operationalised the meaning of concurrency and reflected in true spirit a meaningful partnership between the Centre and the States and at the same time placed on the Union Government the responsibility of ensuring the national and integrated character of education, maintaining quality and standards, requirements for advanced study, international aspects of education, cultural and human resource development. This policy document was reviewed by a Committee under the Chairmanship of Shri Acharya Ramamurti, which submitted its report in December 1990 on alternative modalities of implementation.

The N. Janardhana Reddy Committee set up by the CABE again reviewed the Policy in 1992. The Committee recommended a revision of the Programme of Action (POA) and laid special emphasis on education for women's equality, education for SCs/STs, and educationally backward minorities. The NPE and its POA were adopted in 1992. Over the years, a number of programmes have been taken up In the true spirit concurrently between the Union Government and the States. Mention may be made of programmes like Operation Blackboard, Non-formal Education, establishment of District Institutes of Education and Training (DIETs), National Literacy Mission, Scheme of Nutritional Support to Primary Education (Mid-day Meals), District Primary Education Programme (DPEP), Vocational Education, Cultural and Value Education, Environmental Education, Improvement of Science Education in Schools, Educational Technology, Computer Literacy and Studies in Schools, Community Polytechnics and such like..

Programmes

The most critical area here is elementary education which currently absorbs about 50% of plan funds for education as a whole. Among the more important schemes, mention may be made of 'Operation Blackboard' which aims at qualitative improvement of primary schools by providing two reasonably large all-weather rooms along with separate toilet facilities for boys and girls and at least two teachers, one of them being preferably a woman. Provision of essential teaching and learning material including blackboard, maps, charts, a small library, toys and games and some equipment for work experience is also part of the scheme. The scheme has now been operational since 1987-88. 5.22 lakh primary schools have already been covered under the scheme which has now been expanded to the upper primary school system where 47,000 schools have been covered. 1.8 lakh additional teachers have also been provided for and 1.72 lakh school rooms constructed.

The District Primary Education Programme (DPEP) is also one of the major interventions in the field of primary education. It is currently operational in 54 districts of different states and 60 more districts are expected to be brought under its purview soon. The DPEP is a multifaceted holistic programme based on principles of decentralisation and community initiative in the sphere of primary education. Low female literacy districts are focussed upon, the other factor being districts where the total literacy campaign have been successful.

For those out of school, the Programme of Non-formal Education is also an integral part of the strategy to achieve universal elementary education. The Programme was started in 1979 to cover those out of school in educationally backward states. It has now been extended to cover urban slums, tribal areas, hilly and desert areas with a special emphasis on working children. The Programme now covers 21 States/UTs. 2.79 lakh NFE centres have been sanctioned out of which 38,000 centres are being managed by 544 Non-Governmental Organisations.

The National Programme of Nutritional support to Primary Education, popularly known as the Mid-day Meal Scheme is also a major intervention for increasing enrolment and retention in schools. The programme which was started on 15th August, 1995 will cover 11 crore children studying in classes I to V by 1997-98. Cooked meals are supposed to be served in schools. However, States have the flexibility to distribute foodgrain at the rate of 3 kg. per child per month.

In the domain of adult education, the National Literacy Mission alms to cover 100 million illiterates by 1998-99 and to make the nation fully literate by 2005 A.D. Literacy campaigns have been extended to cover 417 districts and post-literacy campaigns to sustain the impact will cover 178 districts. Under the National Literacy Mission, 58 million persons have been made literate so far.

Teacher training which is a critical input in quality education and in achieving universal elementary education had been given due importance under the National Policy on Education, 1986. The principal institution at the grass roots level for providing pre-service and in-service training to school teachers was to be the District Institutes of Education and Training. 424 DIETs have been sanctioned so far and 4.5 lakhs teachers covered under the special orientation programme for primary teachers. The training has been principally in the matter of use of Operation Blackboard material as also orienting them towards the minimum levels of learning strategy. At the apex level,, the National Council of Teacher Education has been set up as a statutory body to plan and co-ordinate development of teacher education systems as also for regulation and maintenance of norms and standards in teacher education.

At the secondary level an important intervention has been in the vocationalisation of education for which the scheme of vocationalisation of secondary education was introduced in February, 1988 with the three-fold objective of enhancing individual employability, reduction of the mismatch between demand and supply of skilled manpower and to provide all alternative to those pursuing higher education without particular interest or purpose. The Programme is being implemented by all the States/UTs (except Lakshadweep). Up to the end of 1995-96, 18,709 vocational sections had been approved in 6,476 schools, creating capacity for diversion of 9.35 lakhs students which is I I% of the enrolment at the +2 level. Vocational courses are to be introduced based on an assessment of local manpower requirement. About 150 vocational courses have been introduced in six major areas, viz., Agriculture, Business and Commerce, Engineering and Technology, Health and Para-Medical services, Home Science, Services and others.

There has been considerable advance in the techno-economic sector coupled with investment in the technical education system. With a view to bringing the benefits of such advances to remote and inaccessible areas, the Department of Education has been running the scheme of Community Polytechnics. This is being implemented through a network of 373 polytechniques and a large number of village extension services, which are proposed to be further expanded. About 4.5 lakhs of people in the rural areas have been trained. There has also been a sizeable component of self-employment through this scheme.

The National Policy on Education and its accompanying Programme of Action has given emphasis on the education of minorities, weaker sections of society and those physically handicapped. Schemes have been drawn up with an exclusive focus in these areas. Mention may be made of the Area Intensive Programme for Educationally Backward Minorities, which provides infrastructural support at the primary, upper primary and secondary levels in 331 minority concentration blocks, identified as such by the Ministry of Welfare.

There is also the scheme for modernisation of Madarsas by Introduction of subjects like science ·and mathematics, social studies, Hindi and English in their curriculum. This scheme is purely voluntary in character. Besides, the above, general schemes such as the District primary Education Programme, the Adult Literacy Programme, the Non-Formal Education Programme have an added focus on educationally backward communities and sectors. In the area of higher education, the education of minorities has also a special focus with schemes for remedial coaching, regional facilitation centres and such like.

In all schemes of the Department of Education, women are in special focus. Under the expanded scheme of Operation Blackboard for instance, it is a guiding principle that the third teacher will be a woman. Special financial assistance is granted for NFE centres which cater to women. The DPEP is being implemented in districts where the female literacy level lower than the national average. There is also the Mahila Samakhya Project which deals with the entire gamut of women's empowerment. Free education is provided to girls in Kendriya Vidyalayas and Navodaya Vidyalayas.The enrolment of girls has increased from 28% of total in 1951 to 43% of total in 1991 at the primary level, for middle schools it has increased from 16% to 39% and for secondary and senior secondary schools from 13% to 35%.The dropout rate has declined from 71% In 1961 to 56% in 1995 at the upper primary level.

Importance is also being given to implementation of educational schemes and programmes in SC/ST areas. In order to enhance access to primary education, the norms for school facilities a primary school within one kilometre of walking distance and an upper primary school with three kilometres of walking distance are further relaxed. Most states provide assistance to SC/ ST students towards other costs of education such as text-books, uniforms, schoolbags, transport, etc. A fair percentage of SC/ST students are likely to benefit from central and centrally sponsored schemes like Nutritional Support to Primary-Education (Mid-day Meals), Operation Blackboard, Non-Formal Education, DPEP, Total Literacy Campaign etc. Reservations in admission to technical institutions under relaxed norms, priority in admissions to Community Polytechnics, remedial coaching for SC/ST students in' IITs, Regional Engineering Colleges are among other measures for the educational upliftment of SCs/STs.The thrust programmes for the educational development of SCs/STs is provided through special component plans and through the tribal sub-plan. Comparative data of literacy rates reveals encouraging trends.The literacy percentage for SCs increased from 10.27% in 1961 to 37.4 1 % in 1991. Female literacy is also picking up and has increased from 3.29% in 1961 to 23.36% in 1991. For STs also the literacy rate has increased from 8.53% in 1961 to 29.60% in 1991. The female literacy rate for STs has increased from 3.16% to 19% over the same period.

The Department has also been running the scheme of Integrated Education for Disabled Children. Under the Scheme, children who are moderately handicapped are integrated into the general education system by providing such schools with special inputs such as resource rooms, equipment, special education teachers, books, transport allowance, etc. The scheme is at present operational in 13,000 schools all over the country and is proposed to be further expanded.

Education is a powerful tool for the cultivation of social and cultural values in the context of India's pluralistic society. Education also helps to fight obscurantism, religious fanaticism and superstition. There are, therefore, schemes for improvement of science education in schools, environment orientation to school education, schemes for computer literacy as well as for promotion of universal values in society.

The central expenditure on education has increased substantially over the last ten years. The Central plan expenditure was Rs.621.54 crores for the 6th five year plan and increased to Rs.3,036 crores for the 7th five year plan. The outlay for the 8th five year plan increased to Rs.7,443 crores. For the first year of the 9th five year plan, viz. 1997-98, a plan allocation of Rs.4,045 crores has been made. This increasing financial participation of the Central Government through Central and Centrally Sponsored Schemes in the process of education development is in keeping with the spirit of concurrency characterised by ongoing consensual processes and understanding between the Central and the State Governments.

Our Elementary Education System today is one of the largest systems in the world with 150 million enrolments in the age group of 6-14 years covering about 90% of the children of this age group. Gross enrolment ratio at the primary stage has increased from 42.6% in 1950-51 to 104% in 1995-96 and at the upper primary stage (class VI-VIII) from 12.7% to 67.6%.

Side by side with the national effort to achieve Universal Elementary Education by 2000 AD and Education for All by 2005 AD, the secondary education sector as well as the infrastructure for technical, higher and management education are also being nurtured and strengthened. In the secondary education sector, the Government has endeavoured to promote the Kendriya

Vidyalayas and the Navodaya Vidyalayas as exemplar institutions. Curriculum and examination reform are the other areas where the Government has focussed its intervention. India has one of the largest technical, engineering and university systems in the world. There are more than 200 universities and 8000 colleges besides six IITs, five Indian Institutes of Management, besides the proposed Indian Institute of Information Management (IIMs) to be set up at Gwalior. It has been the constant endeavour of the Government to maintain quality and standards in these institutes of higher learning, which are comparable to the best in the world.

Mention may also be made of the 17 regional engineering colleges which have been set up to meet the country's requirements of trained technical manpower. There is also the Indian Institute of Science, Bangalore which is an institution of national importance.

Resource Institutions

In order to strengthen the educational base, the Union Government has set up a number of educational institutes at the national and regional levels. The National Council for Educational Research and Training (NCERT) assists the Union and State Governments in the formulation and implementation of policies and programmes in the field of school and teacher education as well as in devising curricula and preparation of text-books to serve as models. The National Council for Teacher Education (NCTE) is a statutory Organisation charged with the task of regulating teacher education in the country. The National Institute of Education, Planning and Administration (NIEPA) is the apex institute for all matters connected with Education Policy and Planning and has been functioning as a training institute for meeting training needs and imparts training in the Asian and African region as well.

At the secondary level, mention may also be made of the Central Institute of Vocational Education located at Bhopal which serves as a resource center for vocational education Over the entire country. It has been recognised as a UNEVOC centre.

In the field of technical education, the All-India Council of Technical Education (AICTE) is a statutory body entrusted with the responsibility of maintaining standards in technical education. There is also the network of Technical Teacher's Training Institutes (TTTI) for provision of technical teacher's training as also for supervising the work of Community Polytechnics. In the realm of higher education, the University Grants Commission is the statutory regulating body for regulating standards in universities as also for providing financial assistance for infrastructure and curriculum development.

In the field of distant and open education, the Indira Gandhi National Open University (IGNOU) and the National Open School (NOS) also act as pivotal points in what is among the largest distant education systems in the world.

In the field of language development, there are also a number of institutes such as the Central Institute of Indian Languages, the Central Institute of English and Foreign Languages, Rashtriya Sanskrit Sansthan, Kendriya Hindi Sansthan, which promote development of languages in the country.

Protection of copyright and other intellectual property rights has importance in the matter of economic, social and cultural developments and has assumed strategic significance in the present globalised economy and the far reaching changes going on specifically in the context of advent of digital technology which has posed serious challenge in the copyright and neighbouring rights. The copyright and neighbouring rights in India are governed by the Copyright Act, 1957 and the Copyright Rules, 1958 as amended in 1994 and 1996 respectively. India has long accepted international obligations in regard to copyright protection.

India is a leading member of the World Intellectual Property Organisation (WIPO), the UN agency administering the intellectual property rights as also an active member of three major international conventions on copyright administered by WIPO. The stand taken by India on various copyright and related issues influences the approaches of a number of developing countries which took to her as a leader for championing their cause. Recently the WIPO adopted two treaties, the WIPO Copyright Treaty and the WIPO Performances and Phonograms Treaty in a Diplomatic Conference which was held in Geneva in December, 1996.The Indian delegation played a key role in the Conference acting as a bridge between the developed and developing countries and was able to win support for the Indian position which has found reflection in the new treaties.

The expenditure on education by education departments as a percentage of GNP at current prices has increased from 0.68% in 1951-52 to 3.14% in 1995-96, access to education has increased as an estimated 95% of the rural population living in 8.26 lakhs habitations have a primary school within a walking distance of 1 km and 84% of the population have an upper primary school within a walking distance of 3 kms. At the time of independence, this facility of a school was available within a distance of approximately 5 miles. To improve learning achievements the programme of Minimum Levels of Learning has been introduced in most states.The literacy rate, which was 16.67% as per the 1951 census data, has reached 52.21% in 1991 despite the phenomenal growth of population. There has been a substantial growth in technical and professional education.

The Common Minimum Programme (CMP) provides further impetus to the implementation of NPE by laying down specific time bound targets viz. To make the right to free and compulsory elementary education and to make the nation fully literate by 2005 AD.

The nation has set before itself the task of achieving full literacy by 2005 AD.This would mean covering all children within the age group of 6-14 upto class VIII level either through the school system or by non-formal methods with comparable standards. It Would also mean the acquisition of functional literacy by more than 100 million adults in the age group of 15-35. Efforts are being made in this direction. Recently, a Bill has been introduced in Parliament to make elementary education a Fundamental Right. Simultaneously, with the Right to Elementary Education becoming justiciable under the Indian Constitution, it would be the corresponding duty of parents to send their children to school. A Committee was set up tinder the Minister of State for Education, Shri Muhl Ram Saikia, to consider the financial, administrative, legal and academic implications this seminal decision. The Committee has indicated that resources to the tune of 40,000 crores would be necessary. The Committee's report is being further processed by the Government.

India has made giant strides in the field of education during the last 50 years, but even a greater task lies ahead. Like Through the Looking Glass', the country has to run very fast to stay where it is and run even faster to move ahead. India's efforts in the educational sector has also to be visualised in the overall context of globalisation, liberalisation and privatisation. It is also to be seen in the context of India's neighbours in the South-East Asian region where achievements in the field of literacy have been dramatic. Nothing less than a whole-hearted national effort both in the public and private sectors would be necessary if India is to emerge as a fully literate and economically vibrant nation in the 21st century.

Calendar of Activities for Golden Jubilee

Department of Education

Department of Education -A Bird's Eye View

On 29th August, 1947, the Department of Education became the Ministry of Education under a Cabinet Minister, Maulana Abul Kalam Azad. The Department of Education, which was created in 1910, acquired its new role after Independence. In the Post-Independence period, the Ministry of Education has undergone some metamorphosis both in its nomenclature and responsibilities. The Ministry of Education created 1947 continued until April, 1957, when for the First time two subjects "Education" and "Scientific Research" were brought under one Ministry named the Ministry of Education and Scientific Research.

A new Ministry of Education and Scientific Research was organised into three Departments, viz., Department of Education, Department of Scientific Research & Technical Education and Department of Culture Activities & Physical Education. In 1958, the Ministry of Education and Scientific Research was bifurcated into the Ministry of Education and the Ministry of Scientific Research and Cultural Affairs. The new Ministry of Education took over all the functions of erstwhile Department of Education in the erstwhile Ministry of Education and Scientific Research and the Subject of Physical Education from the Department of Culture.

In 1963 these two Ministries were unified with two departments, viz., Department of Education and Department of Science. These two departments were however abolished in March, 1964 and the Ministry was reorganised in five Bureaus. In 1969, the Ministry of Education was renamed as the Ministry of Education and Youth Services mainly with the objective of paying greater attention on the development of youth, especially those who were outside the educational institutions. In 1971, the Ministry was renamed as the Ministry of Education and Social Welfare. In 1979, the Department of Social Welfare became independent and the new Ministry of Education and Culture was born. Subsequently in 1984 the Department of Culture was separated from Education.

The present Ministry of Human Resource Development was created on 26th September, 1985 by clubbing five departments, VIZ., Department of Education, Department of Culture, Department of Arts, Department of Youth Affairs & Sports and Department of Women's Welfare. Thus, hitherto Ministry of Education now became a constituent Department under the new dispensation.

Organisation Structure

The Department of education is under the overall charge of the Minister of Human Resource Development. He is assisted by one Minister of State. The Secretariat of the Department is headed by the Secretary, who is assisted by an Additional Secretary and Joint Secretaries/joint Educational Advisors. The Department is organised into Bureaus, Divisions, Branches, Desks, Sections and Units. Each Bureau is under the charge of a Joint Secretary/joint Educational Advisor assisted by Divisional Heads.

Functions

Education is a concurrent subject. Concurrency implies a

meaningful partnership between the Union Government and the States.

— Education Department deals with all stages of general and technical education, i.e. school and university.

— In addition it also deals with:

— Department of Education is the nodal department for two major UN Organisations.

— Department operates most of the programmes through:

(a) Subordinate offices; and

(b) State Government organisations.

Non-governmental Voluntary Organisations are involved in a large measure in Elementary Education (Non-formal Education), Adult Education and Language development besides to a lesser extent in handicapped education, minorities' education, etc.

The most important advisory body, which helps for federal consideration, is the Central Advisory Board of Education (CABE). Minister of Human Resource Development is the Chairman of this Board. All State Education Ministers, elected members of Parliament and nominated academics are members of the Board.

Elementary Education

1. Amendment of Constitution of India to make the right to free and compulsory education from 6-14 years a Fundamental Right and Fundamental Duty. The Constitution 83rd Amendment Bill has been introduced in Rajya Sabha on 28.7.97.

2. Establishment of National Elementary Education Mission (NEEM) to achieve goal of Universalisation of Elementary Education WEE) before we enter into 21st Century.

3. Launching of National Media & Advocacy Campaign for achieving UEE.
4. Initiating pilot project in collaboration with M/s Sulabh International, Govts. of Bihar and Haryana for construction of toilet for girls in rural areas.

Adult Education

All the States/UTs have been advised to organise activities right from the village to the State level on Independence Day, 1997 to activate the literacy campaign. These activities include Kala jathas and Literacy-cum-cultural processions at the village level; essay competitions, painting competitions, district administration organised processions and rallies etc. at the district level and literacy rallies presided over by the Chief Minister and Education Minister; Sammelans, Seminars etc. at the State level.

CD ROM Project

The CD ROM will be released around August 15th. It will contain 150 important documents running to 42,000 pages on various sectors of education. The important documents include the proceedings of CABE, Reports of Commissions/Committees like Kothari Commission, Ramamurthy Commission, Janardhan Reddy Committee, Five Year Plan documents, Education Surveys and Statistics, etc.

Special Programmes

On the occasion of the celebration of the Golden Jubilee of India's Independence, an allocation of Rs.200 crore has been provided in the budget grant of Department of Education, out of which Rs.50 crore is earmarked to the Department of Science &Technology. For the remaining amount, the Department. of Education is planning a series of activities to strengthen large number of scientific, technical, and educational institutions as well as specific activities synchronising the observance of the Golden Jubilee of India's Independence. A special package of Rs.9 crore for-Jammu & Kashmir and Rs. 7 crore for the North-East has already been approved in this respect.

University Grants Commission

The University Grants Commission (UGC) was established in 1956 by all Act of Parliament. Section 12 of the UGC Act provides that it shall be general duty of the Commission to take, in consultation with the universities or other bodies concerned, all such steps as It may think fit, for the promotion and coordination of university education and for the determination and maintenance of standards of teaching, examination and research in universities. For the purpose of performing its functions under the Act, the Commission may inquire into the financial needs of universities and allocate and disburse grants to them for the development and/or maintenance of such universities or for any other general or specified purpose. At present, UGC provides financial assistance to Central Universities both for maintenance and development purposes; development grants to 103 eligible State Universities; and development or maintenance grants, as the case may be, to the eligible Deemed Universities. UGC also provides development grants to 4,730 eligible colleges.

At present, there are 166 Central/State Universities, 37 Deemed Universities and 9,278 colleges, out of which only 4,730 colleges are eligible to receive grants from the Commission. The students enrolment in institutions of higher education is estimated to be approximately 64.26 lakh students. The teaching staff strength in universities and affiliated colleges stood at 3.10 lakh at the end of 1995-96.

Major Programmes

A crucial element in the development of higher education is the promotion of research. UGC provides financial assistance on a selective basis, to such of the Departments which have credentials for undertaking quality research or are reputed centres of instruction and learning. Under the Special Assistance Programme, assistance is provided to the selected University Departments at three levels, namely:

1. Centres of Advanced Study (CAS)
2. Department of Special Assistance (DSA)
3. Departmental Research Support (DRS)

All the Central Universities have been requested to organise a meeting on the mid -night of 14th August, 1997, as a part of the celebration of 50th Anniversary of India's Independence. Universitywise programmes are listed below:

Name of the University	*Action Taken*
Indira Gandhi National Open	Vice-Chancellor of IGNOU has constituted a High Level
University	Committee under his own leadership to draw up an Action
	Plan to celebrate the 50th Anniversary of India's Independence.
Pondicherry University	The University proposes to celebrate the 50th Anniversary of
	India's Independence in a befitting manner by organising a mid night meeting starting at 11.00 P.M. The University also proposes to organise two seminars by the School of International Studies.
University of Delhi	The University has appointed a Committee under the

	Chairmanship of the Pro-Vice-Chancellor to chalk out the detailed Action Plan. The University also proposes to have a seminary and lecture series in the University and some cultural programmes in the Colleges of University.
Nagaland University	The University has constituted a Committee to chalk out Action Plan in connection with the commemoration of the 50" Anniversary of India's Independence.
Jawaharlal Nehru University	The University has assigned the task of organising the events in connection with 50" Anniversary of Independence. Regarding midnight celebrations on 14th August all the three segments of the University community are being involved and it will include activities like meetings in the Auditorium, Prabhat pheri, rallies etc.
North Eastern Hill University	NEHU has appointed Mrs. B. Bareh, Deputy Registrar as nodal officer for celebration of 50th Anniversary of Indian Independence.
University Grants	Establishment of three rotational Chairs for research in Commission higher education for which an amount of Rs. 1.50 crores is proposed.

Indian Institute of Science (IIS), Bangalore

The institute is basically a Post-Graduate and Research Oriented Institute and acts as a National Resource Centre. The Institute was established in 1909. It has close research links with Space and Defence Departments. It plays an important role in planning and execution of projects related to Power Sector, Civil Constructions, Communication and Environmental Planning. The Institute has several continuing education programmes that benefit a large section of students, teachers and scientists in the country. The Institute offers various Courses and programmes in all major disciplines of Engineering, Applied Science and Technology including those in emerging areas of engineering and technology. During 1995-96,1,537 students were getting training in various Scientific and Engineering disciplines in the Institute. Admission was offered to 447 students -176 in research, 21 students in Integrated Ph.D., 193 Students in M.E./M.Tech., 57 students in M.E. (integrated).

Super Computer Education and Research Centre

The Cabinet has approved during 1992-93, the installation of distributing Super Computer Facility and incurring an expenditure of up to Rs. 18.50 crore (Rs. 7.5 crore in Indian Rupees and Rs. 11.00 crore in foreign exchange) towards Capital expenses (in addition to Rs.30.60 crore already released for creation of infrastructure and purchase of two support Computer Systems). The distributing Super Computer Facility consists of parallel computing, special purpose parallel computers, Numeric Vector and graphic Computer etc. The significant achievements are as under:

1. Creation of functionally distributed super computing environment;
2. High end super computing graphics;
3. Campus wide high speed fibre; optic network at fast access;
4. This facility is used by several scientists from other institutes;

5. Providing national and international trainings;
6. Undertaken sponsored and consultancy research and
7. Manpower training for Government and Industry personnel etc.

Activities

On 2nd March, 1997 the Super Computer Education and Research Centre was dedicated to the nation by the then Prime Minister. The Programme was dedicated as part of Golden Jubilee Celebrations of India's Independence. Symposium on Research at IISC-Current Status and Future Directions on 15th August, 1992 at Bangalore.

National Council of Educational Research and Training (NCERT)

The National Council of Educational Research and Training (NCERT) was set up by the Government of India in 1961 as an autonomous Organisation for providing academic support to the school education system in the country.

The NCERT functions as an academic adviser to the Ministry of Human Resource Development, Government of India. The main objectives of the NCERT are to assist and advise the Ministry of Human Resource Development, in implementing policies and major programmes in the field of school education. In the formulation and implementation of policies and programmes as well, the Ministry draws upon the expertise of the NCERT to a considerable extent. The Council is fully financed by the Government of India.

To bring about qualitative improvement in school education, the NCERT, has five Regional Institutes and Field offices in major States all over the country, and through them, the Council;

- — conducts, aids, promotes and coordinates research in all branches of school education and teacher education;
- — organises pre-service and in-service training of teachers, mainly at the advanced level;
- — organises extension services for institutions, organisations and agencies engaged in educational reconstruction;
- — develops and experiments with improved educational techniques, practices and innovations;
- — collects, compiles, processes and disseminates educational information;
- — assists the State/UT Governments and State/UT-level institutions, organisations and agencies in developing and implementing programmes for qualitative improvement of school education;
- — collaborates with international organisations like UNESCO, UNDP, UNFPA and with national-level educational institutions of other countries;
- — extends facilities for training and study to educational personnel from other countries;
- — serves as the academic secretariat of the National Development Group (NDG) for the Asia and the Pacific Programme of Educational innovation for Development (APEID), UNESCO, Bangkok; and
- — develops, prints and distributes textbooks.

Activities

NCERT proposes undertaking the following programmes as a part of the celebration of the Golden jubilee of India's Independence.

1. *National Seminar on 50 Years of Indian Educational Development:* The seminar will seek to bring together

scholars to make research presentations on, and to critically discuss the development in every major area of school education, including teacher education, during the past 50 years.

2. *Publications for Students and Teachers:* A series of publications dealing with the Indian experience during the past 50 years, in the field of polity, economy, culture, science and technology. The publication varying in size from 64 to 80 pages, would seek to enhance teachers' and students' understanding of various dimensions of contemporary India.

3. *Study of Students' Perception of Freedom and India's struggle for freedom:* A study, based on an appropriate sample would be undertaken to assess students knowledge and understanding of the freedom struggle and its heritage, their perception of its relevance to contemporary India and their vision of the future development of independent India.

4. *Reprinting of India's Struggle for Independence visuals and Documents and Preparation and Publication of its Hindi Version:* This publication in the English version, was brought out in 1985 and has won critical acclaim for its comprehensive coverage both visually and in words, of every major phase, aspect and dimension of India's freedom struggle. Its reprinting has become necessary due to the first edition of 10,000 copies having been nearly exhausted and the volume will soon be out of print. This volume has, unfortunately, not been brought out in any Indian language. NCERT proposes to prepare its Hindi version and bring it out before the end of the Golden Jubilee celebrations. NCERT will also authorise its translation and publication in other Indian languages.

Central Board of Secondary (CBSE)

The Central Board of Secondary Education (CBSE), established in 1929, enjoys the distinction of being the second oldest Board of Secondary Education in India. The Board is an apex National Body, which substantially upgrades educational standards and introduces innovations in secondary education. The jurisdiction of the Board stretches beyond national geographical boundaries. It has an equally diverse mandate which includes: The conduct of annual class X and XII examinations, grant of affiliation to educational institutions, review and upgrading of the curriculum.

Affiliation

Presently, the Board has 4,587 schools affiliated to it. In order to sustain and upgrade academic standards of the affiliated institutions, the Board has appointed territorial study teams to conduct regular inspections of the schools. Earnest efforts are being made by the Board to streamline affiliation procedures.

Examinations

The CBSE conducts the following examinations

— Senior School Certificate Examination

— Secondary School Examination

— I chance Compartment Senior School Certificate Examination

— I chance Compartment Secondary School Examination

— All India Pre-Medical/Pre-Dental Entrance Examinations

Curriculum Development and Business Education in Schools

The secondary and senior secondary syllabii are finalised

on the feedback and the recommendations of the Committee of Courses in different subjects in order to make the existing curriculum more coherent and homogenous.

Commerce based syllabi at the senior school stage have been analysed in the wake of the liberalisation policy thus culminating into a publication: 'India-New Trends and Prospects in Business Education in Schools'.

Vocationalisation and Computer Education

It is the first Board of the Country to introduce Computer Education at the school stage. Not only this, it also ensures linkages with the vocational courses offered by the Board. Besides providing Computer Education under work experience from class VI to XII, basic computer practices are imparted at class IX and class X levels under pre-vocational education. 'Computer applications' in the vocational stream and 'Computer science' under the academic stream are provided by the Board at +2 level.

Performance Analysis

Samples of answer scripts are drawn from different parts and are studied by experts to identify errors and to specify the remedial measures to be adopted by practising teachers.

Public Relation, and the Redressal of Public Grievances

Maintaining effective and credible communication with the public is intrinsic to the overall performance of the Board. Different kinds of publicity material are prepared and produced regularly by the Board. Information is disseminated through print and live media, to create mass awareness, and redressal of grievances remains a high priority of the Board.

Activities

School Level

1. Essay writing competition (English and Hindi)
2. Elocution competitions (Primary, Middle, Secondary and Senior School levels)
3. Posters competition (Primary, Middle, Secondary and Senior School levels)
4. Classical Music -Vocal, Karnataka and Hindustani
5. Classical Music -Percussion
6. Quiz Competition pertaining to Indian Heritage and History

National Level

1. Dr. Zakir Hussain Memorial Lectures [Four lectures (one per quarter) by an eminent Educationist]
2. A symposium on emergent trends in Science Education for Principals and
3. An Orientation Programme for Principals on Indian values and heritage with specific reference to:
   (a) Literature
   (b) Art and architecture
   (c) Music and Dance
   (d) Philosophical bases of Indian Culture.
4. Preparation of compendium of national songs in all Indian languages (preparation for books and audio cassettes songs by children)
5. Special digest of Cenbosec (a home magazine) reflecting the growth and contribution of Central Board of Secondary Education during the post-independence session)

6. Regional cultural meets in all the six regions of the Board.
7. Golden Jubilee Sports Meet of CBSE students.
8. Regional level exhibitions reflecting the struggle of independence and contribution of freedom fighters.
9. Regional Sahodaya School Conference to focus academic issues of the country at the secondary school level.

Kendriya Vidyalaya Sangathan (KVS), New Delhi

Govt. of India approved the scheme of Kendriya Vidyalayas in 1962 on the recommendations of the Second Central Pay Commission, with the idea of encouraging the growth of Secondary Schools with a common syllabus and medium of instruction for providing uninterrupted education to the children of Central Government employees who are liable to frequent transfers. Initially, 20 regirnental schools in different states were taken over as Central Schools. In 1965, an autonomous body, called the KVS was set up to run these Vidyalayas. Over the years, the number of Kendriya Vidyalayas increased to 858 at present.

Salient features

Kendriya Vidyalayas have been set up with the following salient features:

— Kendriya Vidyalayas are fulfilling their commitment to provide educational needs of the transferable Central Govt. employees to a large extent.

— Preference in admission is given to children whose parents had a large number of transfers during the preceeding seven years.

— All Kendriya Vidyalayas are co-educational and composite.

— Common Text Books, bilingual medium of instruction, i.e. English and Hindi and common curricula are followed.

— All Kendriya Vidyalayas are affiliated to Central Board of Secondary Education.

— Teaching of Sanskrit from Class V to IX is compulsory. However, the student can offer Sanskrit as an additional optional subject at Class X also.

— The quality of teaching is kept high by maintaining a proper teacher-pupil ratio.

— No tuition fee is charged from students upto class VII. The wards of staff of KVS, SC/ST, children of officers and men of the Armed Forces killed or disabled during hostilities in the wars of 1962, 1965 and 1971 against China and Pakistan and girl students are exempt from paying tuition fee upto class XII.

Navodaya Vidyalaya Samiti (NVS), New Delhi

In order to provide high quality modern education to the talented children predominantly from the rural areas, without regard to their socioeconomic conditions, Government of India launched the scheme to establish one Navodaya Vidyalaya in each district of the country. Navodaya Vidyalayas are fully residential co-educational institutions providing education upto Senior Secondary stage. Education in Navodaya Vidyalayas including boarding and lodging, textbooks, uniforms etc. is free.

Admission

Admission in Navodaya Vidyalayas is made at the level of Class-VI through a test conducted by NCERT in the concerned district in which all children who have passed

Class-V from any of the recognised schools in the district are eligible to appear.

National Book Trust (NBT)

The National Book Trust, India (NBT), an autonomous organisation under the Department of Education, was set up in 1957 to promote books, habit of reading and fostering book mindedness among people. The activities of NBT include (i) publishing (ii) promotion of Indian books abroad (iii) promotion of books and reading (iv) assistance to authors and publishers and (v) promotion of childrens' literature. The NBT publishes books for general readers on a variety of subjects in various languages like Assamese, Bengali, English, Gujarati, Hindi, Kannada, Malayalam, Marathi, Oriya, Punjabi, Tamil, Telugu and Urdu at an affordable price. The trust also provides financial assistance to authors, illustrators for bringing out reasonably priced text books and reference books for the diploma, undergraduate and post-graduate levels and also for publication of books for children and new-literates. It also promotes books and cultivates the book reading habit all over the country by (a) organising book fairs, festivals and exhibitions; (b) holding seminars, symposia and work-shops; (c) providing financial assistance for organising book fairs and exhibitions; (d) sponsoring celebration of National Book Week; and (e) setting up of Readers' club in schools. The Trust also promotes indian books abroad by organising India's participation in International Book Fairs and organising exhibitions of select Indian publications brought out by various Indian Publishers.

Activities

The National Book Trust is bringing out a publication by bringing together 74 major titles from different languages, which will be labelled "Freedom Package". Books will be released on 14th of November, 1997

Seminar

It is proposed to organise a one day seminar on Copyright Enforcement in Delhi in the second week of January, 1998 The participants will be State Home Secretaries, Director General of Police, Representatives of collective Administration Societies. The Seminar is being proposed in view of the importance of Copyright Enforcement in international trade and economic relations.

National Bal Bhavan

The National Bal Bhavan has been contributing towards enhancing creativity amongst children in the age group of 5-16 years, especially from the weaker-sections of the society. Over the years, the Bal Bhavan Movement which focuses on providing opportunities for creative coCurricular activities ranging from creative/performing arts, environment, astronomy, photography, integrated activities, physical activities to science-related activities in joyful manner, has been expanded to other States and Union Territories also. Presently there are 67 Bal Bhavans in different States/UTs which are affiliated to the National Bal Bhavan, New Delhi. In order to facilitate and reach out to a larger number of children, there are 52 Bal Bhavan Kendras in different localities of Delhi and two Jawahar Bal Bhavans in Srinagar and Mandl. Keeping in view the nature of activities of this organisation and with a view to project the unique national identity to this institution, Bal Bhavan Society of India has been renamed as National Nil Bhavan during last year.

The National Bal Bhavan has thus been functioning as a Resource Centre to enhance skills of teachers in identifying and nurturing creativity of children and providing opportunities to children directly to further their creativity; and as a nodal agency for providing guidelines, academic support and technical know-how to affiliated Bal Bhavans.

Activities

31st July' 97

As a pre Independence day celebration Bal Bhavan had a tree plantation when 50 plants were planted by children & staff amidst mass singing. Each plant is to be adopted by an activity section in order to nurture it.

August'97 : 8th -11th August: A workshop cum camp on 'The First Freedom Movement-1857'

13th August: Games for children & staff

14th August: Mass tree plantation at the Delhi Ridge

15th August: Flag hoisting at National Bal Bhavan, Rural Bal Bhavan Mandi & 52 Bal Bhawan Kendras, Tri colour Kite Flying Activity

19th -23rd August: Mithila Painting workshop with the objective of integration, conservation, use of natural resources & awareness about our traditional folk art.

27th -28th August: Orientation Programme for Resource Persons & School Teachers on Innovative Methods of Teaching Curriculum Based Science.

September'97 : 12th -13th Sept.: National Literacy Meet 'Adhi Sadi Ka Bachpan' A discussion on Achievements, Developments & Advancements in the field of Children's Literature during the 50 years of independent India and social emotional, educational, psychological and economical problems etc. of children. Also in the month of September there will be a Symposium on the 'Era of Social Reforms'. The period of social reforms was significant because the backwardness of Indian society was due to the prevalent social ills and lack of modern education. This backwardness was further intensified by the British regime. A need was thus felt to awaken the masses through a social awakening movement spearheaded by religious reformers.

October'97 : Symposium on 'Mahatma Gandhi' to commemorate his birth anniversary.

November'97 : 14th -19th Nov.: National Integration Camp and Children's Assembly in keeping with the 50th Anniversary of independence will be targeted towards inculcating national values of Integration & Universal Brotherhood the main theme of Integration Camp would be Hum Aur Hamari Swadhinata'

December'97 : Kavi Sammelan will be organised wherein children dressed like noted poets would read out the poems of the great poets. These poems will not only glorify our motherland but also instill patriotic fervour.

National Conference of Young Environmentalists: To acquaint the children with the natural resources of our country they will be taken to Diu/Dwarka for a National Camp. Environmental protection and dependence of man on environment is the main theme of the camp.

January'98 : To celebrate the Birth Anniversary of Subhash Chandra Bose the children of Rural Bal Bhavan Mandl will take out a 'Prabhat Pheri'. This march will also commemorate the Indian national Army's attack on North Eastern parts of India to liberate the country from the British regime.

Bal Bhavan intends to take part in the Republic Day Parade in January'98 wherein a tableau depicting the multifarious activities of Bal Bhavan will be projected.

Feburary'98 : Bal Bhavan Kendra Divas: Thousands of children from 52 Bal Bhavan Kendras located in slums, resettlement colonies, remand homes, MCD/NDMC schools, community centres will take part in a grand 'Mela'. The theme of the mela Would be '50 years of India's Independence'. During this mela the children will also enact a skit on the Simon Commission's arrival in India and other related issues.

March'98 : A photo exhibition depicting India's progress and developments during the 50 years will be put up. These photographs will be taken, developed and enlarged by Bal Bhavan children.

April'98 : A nukkad natak on the Jalianwalan Bagh Massacre will be enacted at Bal Bhavan by the Senior Repertory section and the same will be taken to different schools.

May -June'98 : During the summer months thousands of children come to Bal Bhavan. Special programmes, workshops such as Bank illustration Workshop, Video Workshops, Science Workshop, Innovative Board Games, Paper Sculpture Workshop etc. will be organised during this period. The theme of this year's programmes would be 50 years of India's Independence. The dates of these programmes will be finalised later.

As Pakistan and Bangladesh were both an integral part of India before independence, we would take up these two countries as subjects of a workshop. The basic emphasis would be on inculcating a feeling of universal brotherhood among children.

July'98 : During the month of July we propose to assimilate and amalgamate the feed back from extension projects i.e. 52 Bal Bhavan Kendras and 70 affiliated State Bal Bhavans. During the National Bal Shree Camp when children from all the states will assemble in Delhi we will have one day celebration wherein special efforts would be made to commemorate 50 years of India's Independence.

August'98 : National Literacy Meet would be held in the month of August. The book on 'Adhi Sadi Ka Bachpan' would be released on this occasion.

'Quit India Resolution' was passed in the month of August, 1942. To commemorate this challenge to the British Raj an exhibition on freedom movement as a whole will be put up. Symposiums, workshops and skits will also be taken up.

On 15th August' 98 during the grand finale all the children of the National Bal Bhavan, Bal Bhavan Kendra, Rural Bal Bhavan, Mandi will assemble at National Bal Bhavan for a befitting closing ceremony.

Central Institute of English and Foreign Languages (CIEFL)

In order to bring about substantial improvement in the standards of teaching/learning of English, the Government is giving assistance through the Central Institute of English and Foreign Languages (CIEFL), Hyderabad for the setting up of at least one district centre for English Language in each State. 26 District Centres were initially sanctioned. There were seven District Centres in operation in different parts of the country. The government is also providing assistance to Regional Institutes of English and English language Teaching Institutes of different States through the CIEFL for strengthening them. There are at present two Regional Institutes of English and nine English Language Teaching Institutes.

Books of reference, descriptive catalogues of rare manuscripts, self instruction manuals for teaching languages, original writings on Linguistics, Literacy, Indological, Social, Anthropological and cultural themes, critical editions and/or publication of old manuscripts with or without translations, transliteration and publication of classics from an Indian Language in to

English, reprint /revised editions of rare books published more than 30 years ago and remaining out of print and any other publication as may be individually accepted as conducive to the promotion of an Indian language qualify under the relevant schemes.

Activities

Freedom 50-community sports and games, cultural programme, fire works etc. to be held on 14-15th August, 1997.

National Council for Promotion of Urdu Language (NCPUL)

The Government has constituted the National Council for Promotion of Urdu Language (NCPUL) as an autonomous body to replace the Taraqi-e-Urdu Board with a view to further broad-basing Urdu promotional activities.The NCPUL has become functional w.e.f. 1st April, 1996. From the same date the Taraqi-e-Urdu Board has ceased to exist.

The NCPUL is engaged in preparation of academic lectures in Urdu for the benefit of Urdu speaking people of the country. Financial assistance is provided to 48 Calligraphy Training Centres spread in different parts of the country. Out of the 12 volumes of Urdu Encyclopaedia planned to be published, the first volume has been published and others are under preparation.

National Council for Promotion of Sindhi Language (NCPSL)

The Government has constituted the National Council for Promotion of Sindhi Language as an autonomous body with its Headquarters at Vadodara for promotion and development of Sindhi Language. The Minister for Human Resource Development is the Chairman of the Council.

Activities

Several programmes for development of Sindhi Language were assisted during the year by the Sindhi Unit of Central Hindi Directorate.

Conference on Development of Sindhi to be held at Vadodara in December, 1997 Central Hindi Directorate (CHD)

The Central Hindi Directorate was set up in March, 1960 as a subordinate Office of the Ministry. The Directorate has since been implementing a number of schemes for the promotion and development of Hindi.

The Directorate is engaged in the task of preparation of Hindi and Regional language based bilingual, trilingual and multilingual dictionaries. So far, the Directorate has brought out 13 Hindi based bilingual and 30 other bilingual and trilingual dictionaries. The Directorate also undertook the projects of Czech-Hindi, German-Hindi, Hindi-Chinese, Hindi-Arabic, Hindi-French and Hindi-Spanish dictionaries, which have successfully been completed. The Directorate has also brought out 11 Conversational Guides for non-Hindi speaking Indian students and a Hindi Primer (in four parts) for foreigners. A project of bilingual dictionaries of the languages of the neighbouring countries has also been undertaken by the Directorate, which is in progress. The Dictionaries of Hindi-Persian, Hindi-Indonesian, Hindi-Sinhalese and Hindi-Sanyukta Rashtra Bhasha Kosha are under publication. The conversation guides of Hindi-Tamil, Hindi-Malayalam, Malayalam-Hindi, Bangla-Hindi are also under publication.

The Directorate is also teaching Hindi as a second and foreign language to non-Hindi speaking Indians and foreigners through correspondence course through the medium of English, Tamil, Malayalam and Bangla.

The other schemes which are being operated by the Directorate are (i) awards to the Hindi writers of non-Hindi speaking States; (ii) extension programmes in non-Hindi speaking States; and (iii) free distribution of Hindi books to the libraries/schools/colleges located in non-Hindi speaking States/UTs.

The Directorate is also implementing the scheme of financial assistance to voluntary Hindi Organisations and Dakshin Bharat Hindi Prachar Sabha and the scheme of financial assistance for publication in Hindi. Under these schemes financial assistance is provided to voluntary organisations engaged in the task of promotion and development of Hindi, especially in the non-Hindi speaking States for running classes for teaching Hindi courses of Hindi shorthand and typewriting, running Hindi libraries etc., Limited financial assistance is also provided under the scheme of financial assistance for publications in Hindi to voluntary organisations as also to individuals for publication and purchase of books written in Hindi for the promotion of Hindi. Under these schemes 154 NGOs were approved for financial assistance during 1995-96. In addition to this, 26 titles of Hindi were also approved for purchase.

The Directorate is also having its four Regional Offices located at Chennai, Hyderabad, Calcutta and Guwahati.

Activities

i) Conference on Hindi Language to be held in one of the North Eastern States in Nov. 1997

ii) Special Issue of "Bhasha" Magazine.

Rashtriya Sanskrit Sansthan, New Delhi

The Rashtriya Sanskrit Sansthan established in 1970 is an autonomous Organisation under the Ministry of Human

Resource Development. It is an apex body for the propagation and development of Sanskrit learning in the country. In furtherance of these objectives, the Sansthan imparts Sanskrit studies upto doctorate level through Kendriya Sanskrit Vidyapeethas located in different parts of the country and also takes steps to preserve and publish rare manuscripts testifying to the ancient tradition of learning and intellectual pursuits.

Since its inception, Sansthan has established nine Kendriya Sanskrit Vidyapeethas. Two of these located in Delhi and Tirupati have since been accorded the status of Deemed Universities and are functioning independently. The remaining Vidyapeethas located at Jammu, Jaipur, Lucknow, Allahabad, Puri, Trichur and Sringeri are being administered by the Sansthan. The Vidyapeetha is located at Sringeri and named after late Shri Rajiv Gandhi.

The Sansthan implements a number of schemes for the development of Sanskrit Language.

Indian Council of Social Science Research (ICSSR)

The Indian Council of Social Science Research (ICSSR) was established in 1969 as an autonomous organisation to promote and coordinate social science research in the country. The Council provides maintenance and development grants to several institutes to enlarge the knowledge of social science by improving the quality of research and promoting inter-disciplinary perspectives. The ICSSR has, at present, six regional centres.

The Council has stepped up its activities in academic exchange programmes since 1992-93 with Russia, France, China South Korea North Korea, Vietnam and Japan. The response from participating countries is very encouraging.

Indian Council for Historical Research (ICHR)

Indian Council for Historical Research (ICHR) was established by the Government in India in 1972 as an autonomous Organisation for fostering an objective and scientific approach to the writing of history. Since then it has been promoting historical research in order to stimulate an understanding of the social, economic and political developments of Indian civilisation an the distinctive characteristics of her cultural heritage.

The Council has been pursuing its objectives by funding research proposals covering all aspects of history including history of ideas, of art and literature, numismatics, epigraphy and archaeology, philosophy, science and technology, socioeconomic formations and allied subjects.

6

Programmes of Education for All

A few programmes of high priority which will have to be developed over the next ten years or so to provide good education for all our people and to create a national system of education which will meet the needs and aspirations of the people.

ADULT EDUCATION

Significance and Priority. We shall begin this discussion with adult education (an adult being defined in terms of the Constitution as a person above 21 years of age) because we attach the highest significance to this programme. We believe that illiteracy and lack of 'proper' adult education is a serious impediment. not only to the growth of the individuals concerned but to the socioeconomic development of the country as a whole. We also believe that any investment in adult education, especially of the illiterate poor, will yield quick results in terms of socioeconomic progress and will be extremely rewarding in proportion to its quantum. It is also our considered view that a massive programme of adult education should have been developed on a priority basis as soon as we became free and that illiteracy should have been liquidated within a few years of independence. But this priority was unfortunately not adopted. The

Constitution gave the franchise to all adults, but it made no provision for adult education which would have made it more meaningful.

On the other hand, it adopted the traditional view that we should provide universal elementary education for children in a short period (1950-60) and that the problem of adult education would solve itself over the years. This has led to a neglect of adult education in the post-independence period; and as the implementation of the programme of elementary education itself has been delayed, we have really missed the bus. The percentage of literacy increased from about 14 in 1947 to only about 30 in 1971. What is even worse, the people have not been strengthened and organised to participate in development so that national development itself has received a great set-back. It is high time that these wrong policies were abandoned. We must realise that the programme of educating and organising the people to create a new social order cannot be implemented except through adult education.

Objectives and Content: We believe the initiative in the creation of the new egalitarian social order will have to be taken by the poor and oppressed people themselves. They can effectively do so if they are made aware of their innate strengths and of the exploitative social reality around them, if they are actively involved in socially productive useful work (i.e., are guaranteed useful employment), if they are assisted to create institutions which can give them a sense of self-reliance and a capacity to raise their standards of living, and if they are fearless and organised to resist all exploitation effectively.

The object of adult education of the poor, therefore, can only be to awaken the 'I' and the 'us' in them so that they can assert themselves, both individually and collectively, and to enable them to perceive that they can be free from fear, want, and dependency. We must especially guard against the danger, ever present, that adult education may be used as a tool for educating the poor to their present marginal status, conformity and resignation or for encouraging escapist trends. This does not mean direct political mobilisation which is a task for political parties. But it does mean that the education of the poor must have an essential political component to enable them to come into their own.

The content of adult education of the common people who are mostly illiterate should ordinarily include literacy which is an essential prerequisite for autonomous access to the growing knowledge in the world. But it need not be overemphasized. A literate adult who has a closed mind and does not use his literacy. For continuously adding to his knowledge is no better than an illiterate. It is also necessary to emphasize that the best learning takes place, not in school, but in work and life situations, that learning, working, and living are inseparable, and that each of these acquires a meaning only when fully correlated with the others. This is especially true of adults so that a literacy programme unrelated to the working and living conditions of the learners or to the challenges of the environment and the developmental needs of the country is not likely to enthuse or lead to any meaningful individual or social gains.

While emphasizing the acquisition of literacy skills by the illiterate people, therefore, a programme of adult education must also have a broader content of education relevant to the environment and to the immediate felt needs of the learners and the challenges of improving their own socio-economic status and national development in which they must themselves participate with conviction and enthusiasm. In particular, such a programme should contain an 'appropriate mix' of the following themes suited to the needs of different individuals and groups:

(1) Development of vocational skills to improve earning capacity.

(2) General Education (including health education and family planning).

(3) Citizenship education (including essential political education).

(4) Development studies or a knowledge of the developmental problems of the country in which their own problems are rooted, the role of the people in the solution of these problems and their actual involvement in social and developmental programmes.

(5) Physical education, games and sports, recreation. and participative cultural activities

The programme should also be extremely flexible with regard to duration, time, location or instructional arrangements and should be as diversified as the needs and capacities of the individuals or groups participating in the programmes. Consequently, the planning of the exact content of the curricula needed by specific individuals or groups can never be done centrally. They would have to be intensively local and dialogic in the sense that they should be evolved, in a highly decentralised fashion, by the local worker in discussion with the adults with whom he is working. All that a central organisation can and should do is (1) to create a cadre of good and sensitised workers, (2) to provide them with good training in social objectives, curricular construction, and appropriate methods of teaching and evaluation, and (3) to put out a large variety of well-prepared and tested teaching and learning material from which each worker can choose what suits his requirements best. The critical significance of these central roles is obvious.

Motivation: Adults cannot be made a captive audience and have to be motivated to learn. This will be possible only to the extent they perceive that the programmes offered are of use to them. The best motivation is seen where an attempt is made to create awareness or when the programmes involve them in the solution of their day-to-day problems and strive to bring about some improvement in their life, however small. Good workers who have established a rapport with the people, a well-organised programme which fits the needs and interests of the learners, and good methods of teaching which make learning a joyful, cooperative enterprise between the teacher and students, will be of great help. It will also be of advantage if adult education can be made an integral part of a development programme or a social movement.

Organisation: Perhaps the most difficult and complex issues about adult education relate to organisation: motivating adults, selection and training of workers, production of teaching and learning materials, and, above all, the actual development of this massive programme on the ground. The problem assumes greater significance because it cannot be solved by money alone. There is enough experience to show that, if money is poured into the scheme without the other essential inputs or adequate preparation, we will only end up with corruption and bogus statistics. The non-monetary inputs are, therefore, crucial, not only to save money which is certainly not overabundant, but to save the movement itself. Yet another factor which deserves serious attention is that the adult education, movement can also be used to stimulate the young to national service and to channelise their energies and idealism in fruitful directions and thus make them development-oriented. It would be almost criminal not to explore and exploit the fullest potential of this possibility.

In the light of past experience, we find that three alternative approaches are possible. If quality is the main objective and not numbers, the movement may be organised on a selective basis, by giving full encouragement and providing the needed facilities and financial support in ail cases where one finds dedicated and competent workers or adults desiring to learn. Alternatively, quality can still be maintained and numbers can be increased to some extent, if it is organised as a mass campaign in a small selected area(s) where conditions are favourable. While both these methods are important and should be widely used in the early stages of the campaign, our ultimate objective should be to adopt the third approach and to develop programmes of adult education as a nation-wide movement of good quality. This is the most difficult challenge and will demand supreme skills of organisation, as a mass movement and a massive involvement of all agencies and individuals capable of participating therein.

To what extent can we use the teachers and students in the existing formal system for promoting literacy and adult education? The potential of the proposal is obviously immense because there are nearly 16 million students (from the secondary school upwards) and nearly four million teachers and administrators who can be used as workers for this programme. One view is that the inertia and inefficiency of the system and the class orientation of the teachers and students will make it impossible to work out the scheme in its proper perspective. Another view is that it would be wrong to ignore the formal system altogether, especially because the development of this programme can be an instrument to start the process of transformation within the formal system itself.

Moreover, it may be contended that a massive programme of adult education cannot be developed without fully exploiting the large intra-structure of the formal system. We do not, therefore, think that this is an 'either-or' issue. We must involve students, teachers, and institutions within the formal system of education on a selective and increasing basis. Any voluntary initiative shown in this programme by individual schools or groups of teachers and students should receive due recognition and support. There should also be adequate incentives for individual educational institutions to participate in the programme by linking such participation to developmental grants for buildings, libraries, laboratories, etc.; and it should be possible for students to participate in the scheme and to earn a part of their maintenance costs.

Even the possibility of making participation in the programme obligatory for all teachers and students (as a part of the national service scheme) should be explored; and a beginning in this direction can certainly be made by individual educational institutions committed to the programme. At the same time, we must realise that there are definite advantages in beginning this programme in a big way outside the formal educational system by utilising the large teaching resources, both individual and institutional, which are available in the society and which, though largely unused or underutilised at present, can be harnessed for the programmes. For instance, village panchayats, cooperative societies, youth clubs, mahila mandals, etc., can play useful roles; and large numbers of educated persons who are not professional teachers but who have the necessary enthusiasm and commitment could be selected and trained to organise literacy and other adult education programmes.

All things considered, it appears that we are more likely to obtain the best results only if we combine the various approaches and techniques suitably. The backdrop of a mass movement is in any case inescapable. But against it, we may combine the selective and mass campaign approaches. The workers can be selected, on a large scale, from both among the teachers and the students within the system as well as from the stock of enthusiastic and committed individuals outside the education system, and especially from among the poor people themselves. If anything, the latter may prove to be the better and larger source for the supply of key workers.

In the development of this programme, voluntary organisations will have a significant role to play. Drawing upon non-for-mal resources of society will call for more, not less, organisational effort on the part of government. There should be special schemes to assist them and an adequate organisational effort to harness their services. Institutions known for their competence and commitment should be given a large measure of autonomy to innovate and experiment. Similarly, industry and other employers of labour should be under legal obligation to make their employees literate and, where necessary, certain forms of assistance (such as training of workers) may be made available to them. Literacy and adult education programmes should also be organised for all illiterate workers employed on government projects and development works.

Out-of-school youth (age group 15-21)

What has been said above about the education of adults will also apply, mutatis mutandis, to the education of out-of-school youth (age-group 15-21) which, in our opinion, is the second major programme for the education of the people. The significance of this group is immense (it is about 85 per cent of the total population of this age) and investment in its education will obviously pay rich and early dividends. The motivation of this group is stronger and its educability greater. As peer group learning is very significant, we can effectively use students as well as persons selected and trained from among the group itself, for the development of the programme. Vocational education has a special import for this group most of whom will be looking for a career. We will also have to provide adequate opportunities for continuing formal education, interrupted for various reasons, to all those who desire to improve their career prospects through such education.

Programmes of adult education, whether for out-of-school youth (age-group 15-21) or for adults (age 21 and over), will need the production of a large volume of imaginatively planned teaching and learning materials of the best quality, not only for literacy work but also for post-literacy and follow-up work with the neo-literates. A wide network of libraries and reading-rooms will also have to be organised for the purpose. Effective use may also be made of posters and wall-papers. The universities will have to play an important role in generating materials, conducting research, evaluation, and training of workers. The mass media, such as the press and radio, can play a major role in the promotion of the massive programmes of adult education we have in view and should be fully utilised. The development of the programme in rural areas and for women will need special efforts and emphasis. Needless to say, it will also be necessary to organise a massive programme for the training of workers and to develop a good system of - supervision, evaluation, and continuous monitoring. The programme will have to be launched immediately and will have to be kept up at a very high pitch for about ten years. This is one of the most challenging tasks that education in this country has ever faced.

Universal Elementary Education

We shall now turn to the discussion of the third programme for the education of the people, viz., the provision of universal elementary education for children in the age-group (6-14) with which we shall link the problem of pre-school education also.

Past Achievements and Failures: While we have travelled far ahead of our position in 1947, the remaining journey to the destination visualised in Article 45 of the Constitution is very long and difficult. This will be clear from our achievements in the four specific goals of the programme, viz., (a) universal provision of facilities, (b) universal enrolment, (c) universal retention, and (d) improvement of standards

(1) The first step in the programme is to provide an elementary school within easy reach of every child. So far we have been able to provide a primary school within walking distance from the home of most children in the age-group 6-11 and a similar facility at the middle school stage is available for about 60 per cent of the children in the age-group 11-14. It will, therefore, be possible to realise the goal of universal provision of schooling facilities, i.e., providing a primary and middle school within walking distance from the home of every child within a few years and without much difficulty.

(2) The next step is to ensure that every child is enrolled in a school. The enrolments in 1975-76 in classes IN stood at 66.5 million and those in classes VI-VIII, at 16.5 million. These figures, however, conceal a good deal of bogus enrolment which is proportionately greater in the more backward-States. If universal enrolment in the agegroup 6-14 is to be reached within ten years, i.e., by 1985-86, these enrolments will have to increase to 85 million and 50 million

respectively. in other words, there would have to be an additional enrolment of 52 million in about ten years or about 52 lakhs per year as against an average of about 24 lakhs a year achieved in the past 30 years. This, in itself, is difficult; and it becomes all the more so because the children who are now out of school consist mostly of the hard core of non-attendants, viz., girls and children from scheduled castes, scheduled tribes and other weaker sections. Unless a major effort is made, it will not be possible to reach the goal of universal enrolment.

(3) The third step in the programme is to ensure that there is universal retention, i.e., no child once enrolled in school drops out till he completes the elementary course or reaches the age of 14 years. Unfortunately, a great weakness of the present programme is that there is a large proportion of drop-outs or push-outs, due partly to the irrelevance and poor quality of education, but mainly to the insistence on full-time attendance which is not possible for children of poor families who are required to work. There is clear evidence to show that the proportion of such drop-outs (or wastage) between classes IN and classes I-VIII is very high (about 60 per cent and 75 per cent respectively) and has remained almost unchanged during the past 30 years. The problem of universal retention is, therefore, even more difficult to be solved.

(4) Side by side these programmes of expansion, steps have also to be taken to improve the quality of education because Article 45 implies both a quantitative and a qualitative target. Unfortunately, our failure in this regard is also dismal because standards of elementary education have continued to be unsatisfactory. This is probably the most difficult

aspects of the task and will need the most intensive and sustained efforts.

A New Strategy: The reasons for this failure are both social and educational. There has been a lack of political commitment and the programme has never received adequate priority and resources. Raising the standards of living, over-all development, massive campaigns of adult education, and active involvement of the people are all absolutely essential for its success. But none of these have been given due attention. Programmes of this type have also to be implemented quickly as crash programmes, say, in a period of 5-10 years. But we have made them long-term affairs which have only made the problem more difficult through increase of population, rise in unit costs, and slowing down of the tempo. The content of education has been largely irrelevant and the quality of education, poor. Consequently, the attracting and holding power of the schools has been very low. Above all, the greatest handicap has been the formal system of education which we have adopted: it increases costs through its insistence on the exclusive employment of full-time teachers, keeps millions of children out by its insistence of full-time attendance, and converts the bulk of the children from poor families who are required to work into dropouts or push-outs.

We should learn from these lessons of history and adopt a new strategy to make a success of this programme in the years ahead. Some of its major aspects are given below:

(1) The problem should be solved in a short-term plan of ten years at the most.

(2) At present, we operate on the basis of a system of single-point entry and make fresh enrolments in class I only (at about the age of six years), and expect these children to rise up to the next higher class each

year and to remain in school till they complete the elementary school or the age of 14 years. This slows down the progress very greatly, especially because of the large prevalence of drop-outs. We should give up this outmoded system which does not suit our needs. Instead, we should adopt a multi-point entry and an elastic system of promotions so that even older children who are out of school can be brought simultaneously under instruction. Similarly, we should give up our insistence on full-time education and part-time education should be made available to all children who are required to work and cannot attend school on a whole-time basis. In other words, while the existing stream of full-time education which admits children in Grade I at about the age of six, and takes them up sequentially to class VIII at about the age of 14 plus, should continue. But it should not be the only stream of providing elementary education to children and should be supplemented by three other parallel streams to suit the needs of different categories of children. These will include: (a) part-time education to children in the age-group 6-11 who cannot go to school on a whole-time basis in order to enable them to become functionally literate or to complete class V; (b) part-time education for children in the age-group 11-14 who have never been to school, or dropped out very early, in order to enable them to become functionally literate or complete class V; and (c) part-time continuation education in classes VI-VIII for all children who have completed class V, either on a full-time or on a part-time basis, but who cannot continue to study further on a whole-time basis. These four different streams, taken together, will meet the educational needs of all children in the age-group of 6-14 and bring them under instruction.

They will also solve the problem of non-enrolment or drop-outs and ensure that all children in the age-group 6-14 shall remain under instruction, on a full-time basis if possible, and on a part-time basis if necessary. It is also necessary to emphasize that, for the programmes of part-time education, we need not depend upon full-time professional teachers alone. The large unutilised teaching resources in the community should be mobilised here also as in adult education.

(3) Special attention should be paid to the education of girls and of the children of scheduled castes, scheduled tribes, and other weaker sections of the society.

(4) The massive adult education campaigns recommended earlier can be a great asset to this programme because the education of the parents is the best guarantee for enrolling and retaining children in schools. Further motivational and economic support for the programme would be obtained if simultaneous efforts are made to improve the standards of living of the common people.

(5) It must be realised that the programme can be handled successfully only on the basis of decentralisation. In the last analysis, this programme involves the planning of the education of each individual child (which can be done only at the community level) and the planning of education of every community (which can be best done at the block or district levels). This implies a highly decentralised and yet effective administration far in advance of anything we have attempted so far. A large variety of models is available for the purpose and we may also design our own new models. What is needed is a good deal of innovation, commitment, courage, and firm decisions.

(6) One of the principal reasons which has hindered the progress of universal elementary education is the paucity of financial resources. If this is to be overcome, the unit cost of educating a child at the elementary stage should be kept within reasonable limits through such measures as modification of the wage-structure, adoption of part-time education, and increasing pupil-teacher ratio, preferably through the use of the double-shift system. What is even more important, we must plug the several loopholes in the existing. system which lead to tremendous waste. Simultaneously, we should accord higher priority to the programme so that it gets larger resources, both in absolute terms and in proportion.

(7) The States such as Bihar, Madhya Pradesh, Orissa, and Rajasthan present a difficult problem. They have large populations of scheduled castes and tribes. There are strong prejudices against the education of girls. The number of non-attending children they have is proportionately larger while the overall resources available to them are much smaller. Unless special efforts are made and special financial assistance is given by the Centre, they will not be able to tackle this huge problem satisfactorily. Each State will have to make similar special efforts for its own less developed or backward areas.

Content and quality: The content and quality of elementary education and its universalisation are interdependent. If the content of education is relevant and its quality good, the attracting and holding power of the schools increases and this helps in universalisation itself. Without this support from within the school system, no external effort can ever succeed. Even if it were to succeed, there is hardly any point in universalising bad education.

The basic reform in the content of elementary education is to introduce productive work and social service activities as integral elements of the educational process. This will bring the hand and the brain together and also emphasize social rather than the individual objectives of education. Mahatma Gandhi was absolutely correct when he insisted on this reform as basic to the transformation of the educational system from its middle class to mass orientation. But the introduction of this reform is far from easy. It is not merely a question of training teachers or providing equipment. It is also a basic issue of changing social values and it will not be possible to implement this programme within the school unless we also make a simultaneous effort to make work and social service respected in the wider society itself. It must be emphasized, however, that this reform is meant mainly for the upper and middle classes who have education but do not work with their hands and who consider work-experience or social service as an irrelevant waste of time for their children. Its counterpart for the children of the poor who work with their hands but receive no education is part-time education. We need, therefore, not only the introduction of work in formal full-time education but a large-scale adoption of the system of part-time instruction which will build education round work.

The other major change needed in the curriculum at the elementary stage is to link it closely with the local environment and to make it relevant in itself and not merely a preparation for the secondary school. At present, we have a system of centralised curriculum-construction: the best curricula are supposed to be prepared at the national level and handed down to the States; and each State insists on having a common curriculum for all the schools in its area. Such a centrally planned curriculum cannot provide for local variations and often becomes irrelevant and inert to the learners. Similarly, the curricula at the elementary stage are generally designed to prepare the student for the secondary stage and hence they become irrelevant to the needs of the learners, and especially to the later life of the children, if they do not continue their studies beyond elementary education. If such situations are to be avoided, we must plan the content of education very differently. It should be planned as an end in itself and to suit the local environment, as a result of a continuing dialogue between the teachers and learners. Needless to say, such curricula will vary from area to area, and even in the same area, from situation to situation. What we have to do, therefore, is to decentralise the curriculum-making process and hand down, not ready-made curricula, but the skills of curriculum-construction to all elementary school teachers.

The Common School: As was pointed out earlier, our inegalitarian society has created an inegalitarian system of education which segregates the rich and well-to-do from the poor, the children of the rich and well-to-do attend the minority of 'good' schools which include all prestigious institutions, public schools, English-medium schools, and quality institutions (most of which are private) while the common people have access mostly to the government-supported schools which are generally of poor quality. This segregation must end immediately throughout the educational system. But probably the most urgent step needed is to end it at the elementary stage so that all children, in the impressionable age-group 6-14, rub shoulders with each other, irrespective of social class or caste, and learn and work together. This would be a very effective method of promoting equality, social cohesion, and national integration. We are, therefore, strongly of the view that the common school system must be adopted immediately at the elementary stage. This is basically an urban issue; and strongest opposition to the proposal comes from the top vested interests who use the best schools to perpetuate their privileged position. Only firm political action can break it.

Pre-school Education: Another major reform is to extend the pre-school education, which is now an almost exclusive monopoly of the urban and well-to-do classes, to the rural areas and the poor people. This cannot be done on the basis of traditional models which are very costly. What we need is innovative and low-cost methods that can be multiplied within the available resources. Among these, the following may be mentioned:

(1) In Maharashtra, the training of primary and pre-school teachers has been integrated. This makes two major reforms possible: (a) The play-way methods of teaching can be introduced in classes I and II where they are badly needed and where they help in reducing wastage; and (b) the primary teachers can run, as part of their duty, children's play-centres attached to primary schools (especially in all cases where the instructional hours are reduced to three or four per day) and thus provide some pre-school education to large numbers of children with only a marginal addition to costs.

(2) The Tamil Nadu experiment of using locally available educated women to run pre-schools reduces the cost per child per year very greatly and deserves adoption everywhere.

(3) Child-care can be an important theme round which adult education of women can be built. This will help in improving the home-background of pre-school children and assist in their socialisation on right lines.

(4) Large numbers of women are employed in the organised sector and on several programmes of development undertaken by official and non-official agencies. Arrangements should be made for the care

and education of their young children. The excellent work done by the mobile creche movement developed by the late Shrimati Meera Mahadevan is a good model in this regard.

(5) Above all, it must be remembered that any attempt to draw a rigid demarcation between school and pre-school years will come in the way of universalising elementary education itself. Our primary schools have no pre-schools or creches attached to them. The most common work which girls from poor families are required to do is to look after young children. On the one hand. we are anxious to promote girls' education and organise a number of programmes to increase their enrolment. On the other, we do not permit girls to bring young children with them and request them to leave them at home before coming to school. Since this is impossible, in practice it means only one thing: the girls are prevented from joining schools and there is a positive disincentive in the system against the spread of education among girls from poor families. Experiments have been tried, notably by the late Shrimati Tarabai Modak, wherein. small creches or preschools were attached to primary schools and were conducted by girls themselves under the general supervision of the teachers. The additional costs involved in the programme were marginal, but they succeeded very well in enrolling a large number of girls from the poor families. This idea can and should be adopted on a mass scale.

Wanted: A Mass Movement

Before closing this discussion, we would like to emphasize a point of supreme significance, viz., none of the three programmes of people's education referred to here (adult education, education of out-of-school youth, and universal elementary education) can succeed unless a powerful, nation-wide movement is organised for the purpose and unless a simultaneous effort is made to organise the poor people and to improve their standard of living. This is essentially a package deal and without it we will not be able to meet the requirements implicit in these programmes such as,

— motivating millions of illiterate adults and youth to learn and to acquire literacy;

— changing the motivation of millions of parents and drawing millions of non-attending children into schools and retaining them therein;

— transforming the present orientations of teachers, generally geared to the classes and to the middle class white collar attitudes and changing their values almost overnight, into work and development-oriented ones geared to the service of the common people;

— training of thousands of non-teachers and enthusing them to participate in the programmes and utilising all social institutions also for the purpose;

— organising a big programme of non-formal education outside the school system; and

— taking vigorious steps to transform the existing formal system radically and creating and maintaining a climate of sustained and dedicated hard work, both within and without the school system.

We should also emphasize that even the purely educational tasks, apart from the political and economic tasks of organising the poor and raising their standards of living, are beyond the capacity of teachers as a profession, beyond the resources of the school system itself, and beyond even the best efforts of the entire bureaucratic machine. These tasks can be performed only through a nation-wide social movement in which all the people are intensely involved. It is the responsibility of all the public leadership, and especially of the political leadership, to organise and sustain such a movement at a high level of tempo over the next ten years or so and the duty of the bureaucracy, the teaching community,and all educated persons to support these efforts.

Post Effective Education

There has been a very rapid and unplanned expansion of secondary and higher education during the. past thirty years, not necessarily for good academic or developmental reasons. Some of the demand arises from wrong employment policies wherein a university degree becomes necessary even for jobs where it is irrelevant. A boy often goes to college because he does not get a job when he completes secondary education and a girl does so while she is waiting to be married.

Secondary schools and colleges have becomes status symbols and are often started for the political and economic advantages they confer on their entrepreneurs, without any attention to proper planning of locations, academic viability, or level of unit costs. There is also a built-in element of expansion within the system itself: pressures from the educated unemployed lead to expansion of secondary schools and colleges which, in their turn, lead to greater unemployment and more intensive pressures.

We have also refused to adopt selective admissions and preferred to follow an open-door policy in practice, if not always in theory. Since the available resources in men and money are limited; we create a dual system at these stages to meet the challenges of expansion. There is a core of prestigious and good quality institutions (i.e., institutions in which education is closely linked to good employment) where admissions are selective (and often highly so) and where students are selected on merit which, in practice, implies their ability to choose their parents carefully!

This is surrounded by a large penumbra of poor quality institutions, mostly of general education, wherein the so-called open-door access only guarantees that the child of the common man shall have admission in some institution, however poor, and in some cases, however useless. Ironically enough, this policy of open-door admissions which was supposed to be formulated in the interests of the poor and is strongly defended by them in the name of vertical mobility, mainly benefits the upper and middle classes in practice, and particularly those who live in places where institutions of secondary and higher education are located.

Most children from the underprivileged social groups are eliminated, on harsh economic grounds, at the elementary stage itself; mediocre and third-rate children of the upper and middle classes find easy access to the system especially in -urban areas; and even the talented children of the poor, who are a national asset, often remain outside the system. The direct and indirect subsidies given at these stages mostly go to the upper and middle classes; and the system tends to reproduce an exploiting and parasitic class rather than individuals who will serve the common people. It is these inequalities, inadequacies and weaknesses of the system that we must strive to eliminate or reduce.

General Policy: In the present situation when we are not able to provide even elementary education, post-elementary education cannot be claimed as a matter of right. The policy with regard to its provision should, therefore, be governed by the following principles:

(1) Expansion of facilities in post-elementary education should be closely related to the resources available and the maintenance of proper standards.

(2) A distinction should be made between an individual's right to lifelong learning and the payment of a subsidy from the public treasury for the post-elementary education of an individual. The former is a fundamental human right and no State should have the authority to tell an individual to study thus far and no further. But the State subsidies for post-elementary education should be available, in view of the financial constraints, only to the deserving and economically handicapped persons.

(3) In view of the high priority given to adult and universal elementary education, the resources available for all post-elementary education would be comparatively limited. These should, therefore, be used with the greatest economy and effectiveness, especially in programmes which serve the common people (such as the identification and cultivation of talent from among the poor people) and in qualitative improvement (which is urgent and hitherto neglected).

(4) The bulk of subsidies now provided in post-elementary education, which mostly go to upper and middle classes should be reduced progressively while those meant for the underprivileged groups should be increased.

(5) Even while it is necessary to regulate the over-all enrolments in post-elementary education on grounds of the large and rapidly increasing numbers of the educated unemployed, the access of the underprivileged groups to post-elementary education should be increased so that the new policy of regulated enrolments may result only in limiting

the access of the upper and middle classes to secondary and higher education to reasonable proportions.

Access: In order to increase the access of the underprivileged social groups to secondary and higher education, it is suggested that the type of assistance, which is now provided to scheduled caste and scheduled tribe students at these stages, should be extended to all children and youth from families with an income below a prescribed level, irrespective of caste, religion, or sex. In particular, the following measures are called for:

(1) In all institutions at this level where, for various reasons, admissions are selective, steps should be taken to reserve an adequate proportion of the total seats for the economically handicapped students selected on the basis of merit.

(2) All children and youth from economically handicapped families who are admitted should receive free education, in both formal and non-formal streams. They should be given individual attention and guidance (and other relevant facilities) which will enable them to adjust themselves to these institutions and get the largest possible benefit from them.

(3) The talented children from the poor families get a very raw deal in the present system. Many of them go unnoticed because they do not either enter schools or drop out early. They have access mainly to poor schools which is a great handicap. The culture-loaded selection tests are all against them and they receive little of the personal guidance or tuition they need to overcome their social handicaps. What is even worse, they are often unable to continue their studies because the opportunity costs are very high for them. Well-planned and large-scale

> efforts are needed to ensure that this talent, which is our precious national asset, is discovered and cultivated. At the elementary stage itself, there must be a sustained nation-wide drive to discover talent and selected children should be enabled to continue their education at the secondary level, through such assistance, including scholarships and placement, as may be necessary in each case. A similar programme should be mounted at the secondary stage as well. The selection tests will have to be specially devised to ensure that the talented children of the poor are not a handicap, and they should be provided with the needed personal guidance and tuition. In fact, it should be an article of faith in the new educational policy that all talented children of the poor families shall be deemed to be the wards of the State and shall be enabled to receive the highest education they desire and are capable of.

We would like to make it clear that we do not propose any reduction in the existing programmes of promoting the education of scheduled castes and tribes. These in fact have to be expanded considerably. All that we desire is an additional step, the extension of similar facilities to all economically handicapped students, irrespective of caste, religion, or sex, on the lines indicated above.

Fees: Secondary and particularly university education are highly subsidised at present because the fees have remained low while the costs have been continually rising. As the subsidy involved in this process goes mostly to the upper and middle classes, they strongly resist the raising of fees. In fact, they exert a continuous pressure for reduction or abolition of fees. There is no justification to continue this inequity; and once free education is assured to the poor, early steps should be taken to increase the fees, in both secondary and university education, and those who can should be required to pay for them in proportion to their ability. This a hard political decision; but there is no escape from it, partly to earn additional resources, partly to keep down pressures on the expansion of full-time institutions, and partly on grounds of social justice. Raising of fees to a realistic level should also make students and parents take a serious view of the frequent closure of schools, colleges, and universities.

The problem of high fee charging and financially independent institutions like public schools or some English medium schools is relevant in this context. It is true that there should be no objection, on financial grounds, to the establishment of private or public educational institutions at the secondary and university stages where the fees charged cover all the costs. But there would be serious objection to them on educational and social grounds because access to such institutions would ordinarily be restricted only to the rich and well-to-do who can afford to pay the high fees charged and thus lead to social segregation. The best course would, therefore, be to abolish such institutions. But if this is not immediately possible, the minimum essential reform to be adopted, as a transitional measure, is to obligate these institutions to admit at least fifty per cent students, selected on the basis of merit, from the economically and socially handicapped families, and subsidise such students partially to the extent of the cost per child in similar institutions maintained by the government. This may involve a further increase in their fees which are already high. But the step is fully justified on grounds of equity.

Selective admissions: Should admissions to secondary and university education be selective? The proposal has been stoutly opposed in all quarters and has remained practically unimplemented so far. The principal arguments put forward in its support are three: reduction of educated unemployment; raising of standards; and economy in the use of scarce resources. On the other hand, there are strong pressures for the maintenance of the present policy of open-door access, not only from the upper and middle classes who are the principal beneficiaries of the system, but also from the weaker sections of the society who fear that their chances of vertical mobility through higher education will be considerably reduced if it becomes selective. There is, therefore, no neat and tidy solution to this complex problem and we may have to adopt a pragmatic policy on the following lines:

(1) There should be no selection at the beginning of secondary education (class VIII or IX) because the children are too young.

(2) In all full-time institutions at the post-matriculation stage which receive aid from state funds, proper standards should be maintained and the total number of students to be admitted should be prescribed on the academic basis of facilities available; and selection should be resorted to if the number of applicants exceeds the seats available. In order that this should not adversely affect the interests of the weaker sections, it is necessary to design better and more just methods of selection, and also to reserve adequate seats for all the underprivileged groups.

(3) All non-formal secondary and higher education should receive encouragement and continue the present policy of open-door access. From this point of view, all public examinations at the secondary and university stages should be open to private candidates who have studied on their own. The facilities for correspondence courses (including library and contact programmes) should also be adequately provided in all the linguistic regions.

These policies will ensure that expansion of facilities in post-elementary education will not be at the cost of quality (which is what often happens at present), that non-formal post-elementary education (which can be self-supporting) shall be available to all who desire it and qualify for it, and that selective admissions, which shall be introduced only in state-supported full-time institutions, will not adversely affect the access of the weaker sections of society to post-matriculation education. The programme will succeed better if there are adequate job opportunities for those who are not selected or who do not propose to go in for further education, if the formal and non-formal channels of education are treated as equal in status for purposes of employment, and if due concession are allowed (i.e., in age of recruitment) to ensure that those who adopt a method of recurrent education (i.e., transferring themselves from school to work and vice-versa according to needs) are at least not at a disadvantage in comparison with those who complete their education at one stretch.

Expansion: As most of the evils in post-elementary education (e.g., dilution of standards, over-expansion, escalation in unit costs and waste of resources) arise from the indiscriminate establishment of new institutions and starting of new courses or increasing the number of students admitted in all sorts of institutions without any regard to academic or economic considerations, perhaps the one major step to regulate the expansion of secondary and higher education is to control the establishment and location of new secondary schools, colleges and universities and the starting of new courses or in increasing the intake in existing institutions. Our policy in this respect should, therefore, be based on the following principles:

(1) The improvement of standards in existing institutions should have priority over starting of new institutions.

(2) No new institutions should be started unless adequate resources are available in terms of men, materials and money.

(3) New secondary schools and colleges should be started only in those backward places where the existing facilities are inadequate or where the need for such institutions is clearly justified. New universities should be established only if their need is established on strong academic grounds.

(4) As pressures for the establishment of these institutions often come from private enterprise, it will be helpful to prescribe rigorous conditions for their recognition or affiliation and to insist on compliance with them.

(5) Every effort has to be made to ensure that all secondary schools and colleges have at least a minimum enrolment which makes them viable and economic. The restraint in establishing new institutions, proper planning of their locations, and the rationalisation, where possible, of the existing institutions themselves, will assist this programme by increasing enrolments in existing institutions.

(6) No new courses should be started in any institution unless a minimum enrolment is assured. Similarly, the provision of existing courses should be rationalised, wherever possible, and courses which have become outdated or have a low demand should be discontinued. Programmes of sharing of facilities and cooperative teaching will also be of great help in reducing costs and increasing efficiency.

(7) No institution should be allowed to admit students in excess of those for whom reasonable facilities exist.

Before closing this discussion, we must refer to two major problems that have a strong influence on expansion of higher education, viz., (a) the close and long-standing nexus between a degree and a place in the privileged group or a job in the organised sector, especially under government, and (b) the wage-structure we have adopted for educated persons.

(1) The practice of appointing educated persons to jobs under government began more than a hundred and thirty years ago as a method of encouraging people to go in for the new system of education that had been established by the colonial administration. It worked well till about 1921 because the expansion of jobs under government (or in the tertiary sector for which secondary and university education generally prepared their students) could still keep pace with the output of the educational system. But since then, the undesirable consequences of this nexus have come to the fore. To begin with, it over-emphasizes the bread-and-butter objective of secondary and higher education and makes them a ladder which enables the ambitious to climb into privilege, even as it devalues their academic objective, viz., the production of individuals dedicated to the pursuit of scholarship and excellence. Moreover, the hunt for a place in the privileged sector or a well-paid and secure job in the organised sector creates immense pressures for the expansion of secondary and higher education because they grow more in proportion to the large numbers of aspirants for jobs rather than in relation to the small number of jobs available. This necessarily leads to an over-production of secondary school and college graduates and to large-scale educated unemployment. Instead of dealing with this problem by regulating the output of the educational system, we try to meet the situation by several devious methods such as the appointment of educated persons as teachers within the education

system itself (which only increases the size of the system still further and compounds the difficulties), creation of jobs in the organised public sector even in excess of needs (which is really equivalent to disguised under-employment and leads to indiscipline and waste of resources), and upgrading of qualifications required for the posts without any justification or by appointing persons over-qualified for the jobs (which only leads to a devaluation of education). But none of these methods have helped; and what is worse, they have merely increased the pressures for the expansion of higher education still further, sapped the motivation of the students, created unrest and indiscipline on the campuses and lowered the standards even more extensively. A stage has now been reached when a university degree has become almost the minimum educational qualification for any worthwhile job and, at the same time, the distance between a degree and a job has increased so greatly that the process of hunting for a job through higher education has become almost tantamount to a draw in a lottery.

(2) In the same way, the unrealistic and arbitrary wage-structure which we have created and which is far beyond our economic capacity, has led to yet another set of problems and contradictions. On the one hand, it increases the unit cost of education so that further expansion of education becomes more difficult; and on the other hand. it increases the demand for expansion of education by making each job more covetable. Similarly, it decreases the number of jobs we can create by increasing the investment needed per job while it simultaneously increases the number of claimants for the job through an enlarged output of the system. What is even worse, it disturbs the value structure in the academic world itself. An

educated person should be an individual who values our tradition of plain living and high thinking and who is close to the people and dedicated to their service. The artificial wage-structure we have evolved for educated persons makes them courtiers rather than seers, increases the distance between them and the people, and converts them from servants into exploiters of the masses. It is, therefore, necessary, not only to break this link between higher education and jobs in the privileged sector, but to transform the present wage-structure itself on egalitarian lines.

If these basic problems have to be tackled satisfactorily, the following are some of the more important measures that can be taken:

(1) The arbitrary, uneconomic and inegalitarian wage-structure should be abandoned, in both the public and private sectors. A new egalitarian national policy on wages-incomes-prices should be enunciated and enforced in a phased programme spread over not more than ten years.

(2) The qualifications prescribed for jobs in the public sector should be reviewed and the present policy of recruiting over-qualified persons should be abandoned. In fact, it will be found that, for most jobs a pass at the 10+ stage (or 10 + 2 stage) would be enough. Therefore, persons with higher educational qualifications should either be disqualified for these jobs or the age of recruitment to them should be so fixed that graduates would not ordinarily be able to compete. The private sector also could be persuaded to adopt similar policies.

(3) The present system of giving preference to those who have studied in full-time institutions should be abandoned; and in recruitment, persons trained

through private study or part-time education should receive at least equal consideration, if not some preference.

(4) Wherever possible, the present practice of selecting persons on the basis of formal education only should be abandoned; and recruitment may be made through special tests which are job-specific and open also to persons who have been trained through non-formal and incidential channels as well. The possession of a degree should not be obligatory for appearing for these tests; and the Union Public Service Commission may give a lead by not requiring a degree for all the competitive examinations it holds, including the IAS and other services.

(5) The tendency to over-professionalise (which in turn over-emphasizes higher education) should be curbed; and work and services should be so organised that more and more tasks are done at the middle or lower levels by paraprofessionals or even nonprofessionals.

Secondary Education: Improvement of Standards and Vocationalisation

Improvement of Standards. Improvement of standards in secondary education is crucial to the entire educational system because this stage provides the teachers for the elementary schools and students for the colleges and universities. Emphasis should, therefore, be placed on the improvement of standards in secondary education rather than on expansion. This will involve raising the enrolments in every secondary school to an optimum level where it becomes academically viable and economic, a substantial upgrading of facilities in terms of land, buildings and equipment (these are substandard in a large majority of institutions at present), and faculty improvement. This will need a substantial investment of funds, a part of which could be raised from the community.

A thorough reform of the content of secondary education is called for and will be the most significant programme for this purpose. As at the elementary stage, work-experience and social service should become an integral part of secondary education. A diversification and upgrading of the curriculum is necessary on the broad lines recommended by the Education Commission. Unfortunately, several controversies have been raging at present over different aspects of this programme.

(1) The Education Commission recommended that the teaching of science and mathematics should be improved and made compulsory at this stage. This is being objected to on the ground that it affects the education of girls and the backward classes who are comparatively weak in these subjects. The recommendation is, however, basically sound and inescapable in the modern world. We also do not believe that there is any scientific basis to the argument that girls or backward classes are adversely affected by this recommendation. At the most, they would need some special assistance in the transitional phase. This should be provided.

(2) Some advocate the deepening of the content of secondary education to improve standards and to keep pace with the growing knowledge in the world. Others condemn this effort on the ground that it overloads the children with inert information and tries to convert them into bearers of book-loads or little memory machines. We believe that deepening of content is essential and inescapable. But this can

and should be achieved through better methods of teaching and evaluation rather than through a mere overloading of the curriculum as we have been doing so far. Probably some rationalisation and simplification is needed at the lower secondary level. However, at the higher secondary stage, consideration for standards should predominate. Any attempt to reduce the content at this level to bring it within the reach of every aspirant would be fatal. Instead, we should select only those who have the competence to receive education at this level where the first steps towards specialisation are taken.

(3) The problem of nature of content of the lower secondary stage (classes IX-X or VIII-X) has not yet been resolved. The Secondary Education Commission (1952) recommended definite streaming and the Education Commission (1964-66) recommended an undiversified course, but without a compulsory pass in any subject, the eligibility to further education depending upon the achievement of each student. The latter is definitely a progressive measure and we should gradually move in the direction thus indicated.

(4) Controversies have been raised about the extent to which curricula at the secondary stage should be uniform over all parts of the country. An absolute uniformity is neither possible nor desirable. But it is essential to evolve, through discussion and mutual negotiation between the States, a few broad guidelines regarding (a) avoidence of matters which would impair or harm national integration, and (b) the achievement of broadly comparably standards at the public examinations at the end of class X and class XII which should be regarded as equivalent on

a national basis. In this, the Ministry of Education and the NCERT have a significant role to play.

The principal difficulties in resolving the conflicting views is the unrealistic attempt to create a uniform and rigid system in all parts of a vast and plural country like that of ours. As recommended earlier, we should give up this attempt and strive to create a varied, elastic and dynamic system of secondary education which can be best adjusted to local conditions and needs. The idea of creating 'experimental schools' which can, under certain terms and conditions, be allowed to frame their own curricula, should also be adopted and promoted vigorously.

Vocationalisation: We have been talking of vocationalisation of secondary education for nearly one hundred years; and in spite of all the experiments tried so far, the enrolement in vocational courses at the secondary stage barely exceeds ten per cent of the total. It will be readily agreed that this situation is far from happy and that we should move in a new direction so that the bulk of the students in secondary schools could be prepared to enter the world of work rather than a college or university. This is necessary even in the present situation where only 25 children out of 100 complete the elementary course; and obviously, it will be even more essential when all the 100 children will complete-the elementary course, The basic issues therefore are: who will go in for these vocational courses at the secondary stage and why? What type of vocational courses shall be provided at the secondary stage and how? It is to these difficult problems that we have not been able to find satisfactory solutions.

Let us begin at the end of the elementary stage and ask ourselves: who will go in for secondary education when everyone completes elementary education and the age of marriage is raised to 18 for girls and 21 for boys?

Some may think that the studies at the secondary level are too difficult and may decide to step off. Others may find the opportunity costs of secondary education to be too high and may decide to leave. This situation should be accepted with one reservation, viz., talented children who cannot proceed further due to economic reasons should be assisted to continue their education. Even among those who decide to continue their studies, some may decide not to enter upon a regular secondary course, but to take vocational courses of various durations and to prepare themselves for specific careers. There should, therefore, be adequate provision for such courses which form the first stage of vocationalisation. This aspect has not received adequate attention so far and needs emphasis in the years ahead.

A more serious attempt at vocational education will have to be made at higher secondary stage where a much larger proportion of students may decide to go in, not for the university preparatory courses, but for the vocational courses which would prepare them for various kinds of employment opportunities, including self-employment. There are already a number of courses which begin at this level and prepare for various jobs in the organised sector (polytechnics, most courses in ITI, teacher-training programmes, agricultural or forestry schools, correspondence, type-writing, shorthand, and other secretarial courses, etc.). But obviously the scope of these could be enlarged, especially if we include programmes of self-employment or entrepreneurship, in various fields such as health, agriculture, industry, or management. Considerable work is needed for the designing of these courses on the basis of careful studies of local situations regarding employment opportunities available in the immediate future. The vocational courses may be terminal in the sense that students will step off the educational ladder at these points and enter the world of work. But there should be adequate opportunity and provision for these students to rejoin the educational stream, if and when necessary, and to get vertical mobility. The lack of popularity of these courses at present is also another problem to faced. But let it be emphasized that the extent to which students will opt for these courses will depend upon the development of the economy, the choice of technology the availability of jobs, the narrowing down of the wage-structure between different levels of workers and especially as between the blue and white collar categories, the extent to which we can assure these students opportunities for further education and vertical mobility, the extent to which admissions to the academic course preparatory to the university become selective, and the discontinuance of the present practice of recruiting highly educated persons for middle-level jobs. What is said here will also apply to some vocational courses of a higher type which can be provided after the higher secondary stage. These will form the third level of vocational courses.

At present, most of our vocational courses are school-based and a large proportion of students who join them do so on an experimental basis before they have definitely decided upon a career or have been selected for a specific job. We should like to emphasize that this process, while essential in some cases, is wasteful and less efficient. Wherever possible, we should try to provide post-decision or post-selection vocational courses. In all such cases, there is good motivation and an optimum utilisation of available scarce resources. Secondly, there should be a considerable increase in industry-based vocational courses so that vocations are 'educationalised' instead of vocationalising education. Such a programme may even be made obligatory on industries and certain grant-in-aid made available to them for the purpose if necessary. Thirdly, there should be an adequate provision for sandwich courses and for regular apprenticeship training.

Higher Education and Research

Strengths and Weaknesses. Higher education in India presents a saga of a few achievements and many failures. Its main contribution is that it has helped to create a large stock of high level trained manpower and to build a good indigenous capability in research. We have also some creditable achievements in science and technology and in agricultural, engineering, and medical education which has helped us to develop a modern industrial sector, to promote agricultural development through the introduction of modern technology., and to build up a network of high quality modern health services.

We have also been able to expand the university base and to establish some centres of advanced study in the universities as well as a few high quality institutions of teaching and research outside the university system. But its failures are even greater. The vast bulk of the institutions, mostly affiliated colleges of general education, maintain poor standards and many of them are too small to be academically viable or financially economic.

The enrolments have increased inordinately; and, as the economy has not grown in proportion, higher education converts, on a large scale, the uneducated underemployment or unemployment (which is mute, unorganised, and without a nuisance value) into educated'. urban unemployment (which is vocal and organised and has a great nuisance value). As stated earlier, this also saps student motivation, creates unrest on the campus, and leads to further deterioration of standards. The courses provided are often irrelevant and undemanding and not sufficiently modernised and diversified; the method of teaching over-emphasize lectures and the examinations continue to be external and traditional. The teaching and learning materials leave a good deal to be desired and the continued use of English (over which an increasing number of students has only a limited command) as medium of instruction creates difficult problems in teaching, learning or communication and lowers the standards still further, besides creating a wall between the intelligentsia and the people.

The Continuing Crisis: Perhaps the worst aspect of the problem is the continuous crisis situation in higher education. Over the past fifteen years or so, the university system in India is passing from crisis to crisis arising out of rapid and unplanned expansion, inadequate finances, lowering of standards, agitations by teachers. students and karamcharis which paralyse university life, official and political interference, and weakness of administration (bordering virtually on collapse in some areas) which fails to rise up to the challenges of the situation and is too paralysed to act on sound academic principles by the atmosphere of violence created on the campus by political vested interests, an ill-disciplined minority among students and anti-social elements.

The emergency created a temporary peace in this situation. But that can hardly be called a solution and a tremendous price had to be paid for it in terms of the loss of academic freedom. With the withdrawal of emergency, all the old familiar scenes of unrest, violence, and crisis are again being re-enacted on the campus, especially as the basic causes of the situation still continue to operate. Very naturally people feel more concerned about the dysfunctioning of higher education than of any other stage of our educational system; and this is, therefore, the one area in which determined action is called for on a priority basis.

Desperate situations call for desperate remedies; and some heroic measures are often suggested to improve the situation.

1) The first is the recommendation of the C.D. Deshmukh Committee that a compulsory national service of one year should be obligatory on a student, who has completed the secondary school, before he is admitted to the college. This is a good programme on its own merits. But its contribution to the resolution of the present crisis situation in higher education is at best doubtful. The programme also involves a very high financial investment which we may not be able to afford and requires an immense organisational effort which we may not be able to mount up. On the other hand, both the financial and organisational issues will become much easier if' the national service programme is integrated with the undergraduate course.

2) The second is the proposal that all colleges and universities should be closed for a year and the students and teachers involved in programmes of national and social service in general and in transforming the educational system in particular. The organisational implications of this programme are even more formidable than those of the Deshmukh proposal. It may also be emphasized that the plan will be effective only if it is well implemented and if we are in a position to utilise the services of teachers and students in meaningful and challenging programmes; and it will be equally unproductive or even counter-productive if this cannot be done.

All things considered, one sees no short-cuts to a radical transformation of the system which will have to be attempted through a well-planned, sustained and vigorous programme in spite of all the difficulties involved.

The Hard Decisions: It was pointed out earlier that the organisation of a mass movement is absolutely essential if programmes of adult and elementary education have to succeed. In secondary and higher education, the position is different: no significant improvement is possible at these stages unless some hard decisions are taken, both by politicians and academics.

1) Some of the hard political decisions to be made will include,
   - regulation of the over-all expansion of higher education, the introduction of the system of double pricing under which the poor will get free education and others will have to pay higher fees according to their ability, and reduction of subsidies, both direct and indirect, which go to the rich and well to-do side by side with an increase in those which go the poor;
   - introduction of selective admissions with the necessary safeguards for the weaker sections;
   - adoption of measures which will eventually delink jobs from degrees;
   - maintenance of discipline; and
   - protection of university autonomy and full political support without political interference.
2) The implementation of a national language policy. This is an example of a decision which is both political and academic and where politicians and academics will have to collaborate meaningfully.
3) There are also several decisions which the academic community (which includes both teachers and students) itself is responsible to make and implement. These include,

- — exercise of academic freedom with courage to function as a critic of society;
- — earning and continually deserving autonomy through the rectitude and quality of administration, level of academic performance and
- — the extent of services to the local community and the nation;
- — sharing and passing down the autonomy from the universities to their departments and affiliated colleges which, in turn, should share it with teachers and students;
- — involving students intimately in the entire life of the university;
- — making radical changes in the content of education and in the methods of teaching and evaluation; and
- — creating a climate of sustained and dedicated hard work in the system as a whole.

It is unfortunate that -most of the decisions in these matters are not being made, and the different groups seem to be acting at cross-purposes with one another. No solution of the complex and difficult problems facing secondary and university education can come this way. Progress will be possible only if all the agencies involved -the Centre, the State, the teachers, the students, and the public at large -play their assigned roles with a sense of commitment and responsibility.

The undergraduate stage: With these introductory observations, we shall highlight a few salient aspects of the reform of higher education which need attention.

1) The undergraduate stage is extremely important and it is rather unfortunate that it is being neglected at present. It should receive attention on a priority

basis. The best teachers available should teach at this stage and strive to improve its standards. Good teachers at the undergraduate stage should have the same status as good researchers.

2) Teaching at the undergraduate stage is mainly a responsibility of the affiliated colleges. The UGC programmes for the development of affiliated colleges should, therefore, continue and be expanded. But the problem will not be solved unless the Stage grant-in-aid systems (which provide the bulk of the finances for the colleges) are radically reformed. What we need is a special machinery at the State level to administer grants-in-aid to colleges and to use the grant-in-aid system as a lever to improve standards.

3) It is rather unfortunate that the existing undergraduate curricule adopt an almost exclusively academic approach to various disciplines and ignore the important role a curriculum can play in building the attitudes of students towards the problems of social change and national development. They need to be restructured to meet the diversity of student needs and the over-riding objective of creating a new social order. From this point of view, it is absolutely essential that every undergraduate student should undergo four types of course programmes: (1) a set of foundation courses which will expose the student to such areas as history of freedom struggle in India and other parts of the world, concepts and processes of development, the problems and challenges facing the nation and approaches to their tentative solutions, role of science and technology in development, Gandhian thought and alternatives in development; (2) a set of core courses which will give the student an opportunity of acquiring a broad familiarity with some chosen disciplines including a

depth-study of one or more of them; (3) some applied studies/projects/field activity which will form an integral part of his course programme and will be carried out in the final year; and (4) involvement in a programme of national or social service for the first two years. A judicious mix of these components with obviously provide a more rounded and richer education to the students; and it will greatly help in changing the wrong attitudes which are now developed among the alumni of colleges and universities and orient them to the service of the people.

4) These curricular reforms will succeed and yield the best results if steps are taken side by side to re-orient and improve the faculty in affiliated colleges. An intensive and sustained programme is needed for the purpose.

5) The methods of teaching and evaluation will have to he radically changed, the lecture method which now dominates the scene almost exclusively should be considered as only one of the methods of teaching/learning and the bulk of the learning should be dither self-learning by the students or dialogic learning through seminars and discussions., Introduction to research or a discovery approach and team-work should also be promoted.

Post-graduate studies and research: Quality assumes the highest significance at the post-graduate stage. In a way, the quality of the entire educational system and of most social institutions depends upon the standards maintained at this stage which supplies teachers to the university system itself (and through it to the secondary and elementary schools) and which also provides the senior leadership in many important walks of life. Post-graduate studies should, therefore, be developed only in research institutions, university departments, post-graduate university centres, and selected colleges which can provide the necessary facilities. Research needs to be encouraged more widely, both on the theoretical and applied fronts, the former being essential to develop self-reliance and a meaningful understanding of the natural and social phenomena in depth without which even applied research is neither possible nor worth while, and the latter for policy formulation and solution of day-to-day problems.

There has also to be a close coordination between universities and research institutions which should function as a part of an integrated system of post-graduate teaching and research. In the past, there has been a wrong concept of the roles and relationships of the universities and research institutions, the former placing an almost exclusive emphasis on teaching and the latter on research. This has led to the creation of substantial concentration of scientists, engineers, and research facilities in institutions which can make only a limited contribution to the educational system and to the training of young scientists.

On the other hand, the universities, barring a few exceptions, have lacked the resources to develop their research programmes which also adversely affects the quality of teaching they provide or the problem-solving abilities of the specialists they train. This mismatch between education, research, and development should be done away with and close linkages should be built up between the universities, research institutions, industry, policy-makers, and the public. This will improve, not only the quality of research produced, but also accelerate its more effective utilisation.

Diversification: A basic reform needed is to diversify the models of institutional structures and their relationships. We began by adopting the classical model of university education, an ivory tower institution of well-motivated students and competent teachers, pursuing the study of Western science and literature through the medium of the English language. This model has long outlived its utility. It has also ceased to represent the reality with the large increases in enrolments, sapping of motivation in a very large proportion of students, and employment of underqualified and ill-motivated teachers. Even its 'ivory-tower' character is partly gone because, while it continues to make little contribution to the community around, it is, in its turn, severely rocked by social tensions and turmoils. While some institutions of this classical model (without the over-emphasis on Western knowledge and use of English as a medium) will always be needed, it cannot be the only model to dominate the entire spectrum of higher education. As enrolments increase and the student community gets larger and diversified, it is essential to diversify the institutional models of higher education, and to create new patterns to suit the emerging needs. In fact, we should move in a direction where institutions of higher education will represent a very wide spectrum of which the classical type is only one, although an important illustration.

At present, the universities concentrate only on teaching and research which they regard as their legitimate responsibilities. It is, however, essential that every university should also develop extension as its third important responsibility and give it the same status as teaching and research. Extension must also become an important responsibility of colleges and should be integrated with their syllabi.

It is also necessary to introduce diversified courses, especially those covering newly emergent and inter-disciplinary areas. There should be a much greater freedom to a student to choose from a large variety of courses to suit his interests. This will be facilitiated by the adoption of the semester system.

Decentralisation and autonomy: To improve standards, we must move away from the existing system of centralisation of academic authority and external examinations. The system is not defensible even in theory; and in practice, it creates very dialatory procedures, diffuses accountability, gives the deciding voice to the no-changer mediocrity, and provides an umbrella for a good deal of inefficiency or even corruption. It also creates several alibis, real or imaginary, which enable the wrong type of teachers and institutions to evade full responsibility for their actions, just as it deprives the good teachers and institutions the freedom to take initiative for creative, imaginative, and more fruitful action. It is, therefore, absolutely essential to decentralise authority and confer autonomy, from the university administration to the university departments and from the universities to the colleges. The existing bureaucratic and centralised structures of the universities have to be radically altered to avoid delays, to get rid of the obsession with rigid uninformities, to create an elastic and dynamic system, and to promote innovative initiatives and reforms.

The concept of autonomous colleges is of special significance in this context and implies that the college and its teachers assume full responsibility and accountability for the academic programmes they provide, for the content and quality of their teaching, and for the admission and assessment of the students. Unless this basic condition is first met, it will not be possible to tackle the problem of 'relevance' satisfactorily or to diversify curricula and relate them to local needs and conditions, and what is even more important, to the needs of individual students. Autonoms alone will make it possible for institutions of higher education to become communities of teachers and students engaged in an agreed and mutually satisfactory process of joint pursuit of truth and excellence. It is hoped that the UGC and the universities will grant autonomy to an increasing number of colleges and that we shall gradually move in the direction where autonomy becomes, not a reward for excellence, but the minimum condition for survival.

National Language Policy

A discussion of standards in higher education cannot ignore the problem of the medium of instruction, the language policy to be adopted by the country, and the development of Indian languages. The British administrators adopted English as the medium of instruction at the secondary and university stages; and in spite of its deleterious educational results, the policy at least worked in the larger social context because the British also made English the language of administration, courts, top levels of industry and commerce, and the national press. It took us nearly a quarter of a century (between 1921 and 1947) to change the medium of instruction at the secondary stage from English to regional language/mother-tongue, first giving the students the option to write answers in their own language, then changing and medium of instruction in social sciences, and finally in the natural sciences and technical subjects, never really knowing, whether in this process the text-books come first or the teaching comes first. In the post-independence period, the same 'muddling through' approach has been adopted at the undergraduate stage and, at the present rate of progress, it may take another 20-30 years for the regional languages/mother-tongues to be the media of instruction at this stage. The time taken is longer because the intellectual effort involved is much larger. What is even more unfortunate, the language in top levels of business, commerce and industry, in senior courts, in the national press, and at all higher levels of government continues to be English which consequently still retains its pre-eminent position as language for good employment. This makes the tradition in the medium of instruction at the university stage very difficult and slow.

Yet another complication is the fact that realising the value of English as the language for good employment, the rich and the well-to-do are switching on to the use of English medium right from the pre-primary stage so that the number of schools using English as medium of instruction has increased fantastically in all urban areas in the past thirty years and the craze is now spreading to rural areas as well. The educational institutions using the regional languages (or mother-tongue) as media are thus becoming second-rate, meant for 'other people's children'. The social segregation on the linguistic basic is, therefore, tending to increase, rather than decrease, and creating greater alienation between the people and those who are going to occupy leadership positions in all walks of life.

A language policy in the interest of the people will, therefore, have to be firmly laid down and implemented in a sustained and vigorous fashion. The main aspects of such a policy are:

1) All elementary education should be given in the mother-tongue of the child, except where the mother-tongue is a dialect or language without a script. In such cases, the education of the child should use the dialect or language concerned as medium till a smooth changeover can be made to the regional language.

2) At the secondary stage, the three-language formula should be adopted. In the non-Hindi areas, the formula is obvious: mother-tongue, English, and

Hindi. In the Hindi areas, the official policy is that it should be mother-tongue, English, and an Indian language other than Hindi (preferably one from the South). The policy also allows considerable latitude regarding the time to be allowed for the study of each language, or the standards to be attained. There is hardly any viable alternative to this and it will have to be implemented in spite of all the difficulties involved. In this, the responsibility of the Hindi areas is greater.

3) At the undergraduate stage, the process of transition from English to regional language is already well under way. It must be expedited. From this point of view, immense effort is needed to produce the necessary text-books and other learning and teaching materials so that the standards improve. The academic community must rise to this challenge.

4) At the post-graduate and research stage where the process is mostly of self-learning, there is not much point about a medium of instruction. But education of this level has no meaning if the student does not have a direct access to the growing knowledge in the world in his own field.

5) Every effort must be made to develop the Indian languages which are the languages of the people and the nation. This programme should have very high priority on State and Central funds for education.

6) At the national level, Hindi has already been accepted as the official language of the Federal Government and the link language for the country. Considerable progress has also been made in its adoption and use. But a prolonged period of bilingualism is inevitable. The official view that Hindi will not be imposed on any group or State is absolutely correct. An understanding and patient

approach is called for, especially on the part of those whose mother-tongue is Hindi.

7) English can never have the absolute and sovereign place which it once had in our midst. But it will continue to have a very important place as an international language which provides an access to the growing knowledge in the world. It is, therefore, necessary to redefine the position of English in our society and education. In the past, English has been used to build up social status and economic privileges for a few; and in education, it has generally played a negative role of preventing the bulk of the people from receiving good secondary and higher education. In the future, these roles will have to be totally changed. English will have to be delinked from status and privileges; and it will have to play an enabling role of providing an individual access to world knowledge. This is a service function where the emphasis will be on enabling an individual to acquire as much of English as he needs at any time in his life and not on discriminating in favour of those who know English and against those who do not.

8) It is also necessary to point out that the adoption of regional languages as media of instruction increases rather than decreases the need to study English.

9) Several changes are needed in the present policies regarding the teaching of English in the school system and outside. By and large, no English need be taught at the primary stage. But English should be taught in middle and secondary schools. A pass in English should not, however, be obligatory for a successful completion of secondary education. For admissions to the first degree, a pass in a language test in English should be obligatory. But a student should have the option to pass it before the end of

his first year and adequate arrangements for specialised intensive courses in English (to enable a student to prepare for the test) should be made in every college. At the postgraduate stage also, a student should be expected to have a good working knowledge of English and even of another foreign language, depending upon the field of his study. In addition, there should be adequate arrangements for teaching English through non-formal channels and for adults. The essence of the new programme thus will be to provide adequate facilities to learn English to each group of students or individuals according to their needs at every stage of education and even outside the educational system.

10) Full encouragement should be given to the study of foreign languages other than English and adequate facilities should be provided for their study.

One point must be emphasized. The language problem is extremely explosive. It must, therefore, be approached cautiously and played down. It is only with patient and silent but steady and continuous work within the educational system itself combined with appropriate administrative action (such as to hold all competitive and selection examinations in regional languages) that we will be able to solve this national problem which is often complicated and vitiated by short-sighted and hasty political actions.

Administration and Finance

The implementation of the major programmes of educational reconstruction discussed above will involve corresponding changes in educational administration and a new approach to educational finance.

Leadership: Who will provide the leadership to these programmes of educational transformation? No one doubts that a dynamic leadership is essential for success. But concepts and visions of the leadership needed show great variations.

Can this leadership arise within the educational system itself?

1) The traditional view assumes that the leadership will come from the educational bureaucracy: the Education Secretaries, the Directors of Education, the Inspectorate, and the administrators. The proposals made, equally traditional, include the creation of an Indian Education Service and the strengthening of the State Departments of Education which means more officers who would be more highly paid and more qualified, with more and more of in-service training. While one recognises the useful role of bureaucracies, the limits of this approach are equally obvious. Bureaucracy alone will not be able to plan and implement the radical programmes visualised here.

2) Another view, which is also traditional, is that the leadership will come from the universities. In this view, a key role is assigned to the university departments of education which, in turn, would work with the training institutions for teachers and strive to promote experimentation, innovation, evaluation and reconstruction. The theoretical and practical contribution of university departments of education and training institutions to educational development, and especially to pedagogy, can be very considerable. From the over-all point of view, however, the university departments of education (which, in India, have mostly concerned themselves with the training of secondary school teachers and teacher educators) and the training colleges for secondary and elementary school teachers have made only a limited contribution so far even to the

development of pedagogy. Their contribution to the planning and implementation of radical educational reforms has been even less. These institutions will, therefore, have to change their outlook radically before they can become instruments of change.

3) A third view looks to the teachers and to their organisations for providing the leadership needed for radical educational reforms. Unfortunately, our past experience indicates that neither the teachers, nor their organisations, have shown adequate commitment to radical educational reforms and have not provided any effective leadership in planning and implementing them. There is an urgent need for introspection in this regard.

4) Yet another view suggests that the university students may take the leadership in bringing about radical changes in education (and even in society). Here also, the actual experience in the past has been far from encouraging. It is true that students in higher education often espouse and agitate for some educational or social issues. But these generally have a negative impact on standards; and their contribution to radical educational or social changes of the type visualised here is almost negligible. This also is a case for careful introspection.

All things considered, it appears that the dynamic leadership needed to initiate radical reforms may not arise within the educational system which, at present, largely works for conformity with existing patterns and processes within a social status quo. At the same time, no educational reforms, radical or otherwise, can be put across without the active collaboration of the educational administrators, universities, teachers and students. Under these circumstances, we will have to intensify our efforts to build up and strengthen a new leadership with-in the educational system itself so that radical educational reforms are conceived and implemented. This will require an intensive effort to orient the different groups within the educational system itself to the wider social issues and problems and to the close relationships between educational and social transformation. It is widely recognised that there are several competent and committed individuals in all these four groups - administrator, teacher educators, teachers, and students - who can make a good contribution to planning and implementation of radical educational reforms. But unfortunately, their numbers are small and they do not become effective because of the rigidity and uniformity of the educational system which gives a strong veto to the no-changer or the traditional majority. We must, therefore, strive to increase the numbers and proportion of such individuals and help them to become more effective through the creation of a decentralised, elastic and dynamic structure. What is even more important, there must be a close link between these enlightened workers within the educational system and the progressive forces and workers outside the educational system. It is only this joint action that can yield the best results.

To what extent can the leadership needed to bring about radical educational reforms arise outside the educational system? Since the basic educational issues are essentially political, and since educational and social reform have to be pursued side by side, the leadership for the planning and implementation of these programmes of radical educational reconstruction can best come from the state itself; and the whole programme becomes easier if the state identifies itself with the poor and the under-privileged and commits itself to bring about the complementary and simultaneous social transformation needed. But this 'political will' is often absent; and in such an eventuallity, the needed leadership can only be provided by the political and social workers who are engaged in the education and organisation of the poor and under-privileged social groups. If they start the chain reaction, there would be many kindred and responsive elements, not only within the education sub-system, but in all the social sub-systems as well, which will give support and develop the programme further. The role of political and social workers outside the educational system thus becomes crucial and significant. This is where committed individuals and voluntary organisations have a unique contribution to make.

In the Indian situation, the state has so far identified itself, by and large, with the educational demands and interests of the upper and middle classes and its commitments to promote the educational interests of the weaker sections have been comparatively less urgent and powerful. Under these circumstances, the role of political and social workers who are trying to help the people to come into their own and the individuals and groups within the educational system who are committed to radical reforms becomes extremely significant. They can educate public opinion, bring pressure upon the state, and help to create the social, economic, and political conditions which will make the implementation of radical educational reforms possible.

Administrative structures and processes: The existing administrative structures and processes which have been designed for a uniform, rigid, and static (or slowly changing) organisation of a centralised character have no place in the new educational system which must be highly decentralised, diversified, elastic, and dynamic to suit the needs of a rapidly changing society in a vast and plural country like that of ours. India became free in 1947. But the Indian teacher is still bound by so many official directives, decisions, and orders in all matters including curricula, text-books, teaching methods, and examinations that he has not yet been able to get the fundamental freedom to teach; and if anything, his bondage has increased and become greater in the past 30 years. Consequently, he has also not been able to give the basic freedom to learn to his students. As can well be imagined, the teaching-learning process thus becomes artificial and loses all its spontaneity and creativity under these conditions where both teachers and students have been enslaved to a system. Perhaps the greatest administrative reform needed at present is to give their freedom to teachers and students and make education a creative and joyous adventure to all concerned.

From this point of view, it is necessary to emphasize that a highly centralised administrative apparatus is unsuitable for a progressive educational system for the people wherein the people themselves are expected to participate effectively. It is true that education is a national concern and that we must also have a national policy on education. But whether education is in the concurrent list (which will make the coordinating responsibility of the Centre a little easier to implement) or not, it is beyond doubt that the main role of the Central Government is to provide a stimulating but none-coercive leadership and that the effective authority in education should vest in the State Governments. In fact, it is undesirable to concentrate too much of authority even in the State Governments. We have already indicated that, in higher education, the States must respect the autonomy of the universities which, in turn, must share it with the departments, colleges, teachers, students, and the lay representatives. In so far as school education is concerned, there should be suitable authorities at the district (or block) level and the local community must be associated with its school in an effective way. Care should be taken to see that, in all this process, there is adequate devolution of resources to match the delegation of authority and transfer of responsibility.

This progressive delegation of authority from New Delhi to the village community should be accompanied by greater freedom to schools and teachers who should have increasing freedom to frame curricula, to assess their students and to innovate and experiment. The concepts of experimental schools and autonomous colleges should be developed on as large a scale as possible. In short, the objective of all administrative reforms, as stated earlier, should be to create a decentralised, diversified, elastic, and dynamic educational system.

An important reform which will help and strengthen this process is the system of college-school complexes recommended by the Education Commission (1964-66). The object of this reform is to fink educational institutions between themselves instead of separating and atomising them as is done at present. This view envisages a group of elementary schools working in close collaboration with a secondary school, a group of secondary schools working in close collaboration with a college, and a group of colleges working in close collaboration with a university. The programmes of collaboration will cover, among others, sharing of facilities, identification and development of talent, joint teaching and allied activities and better provision for inservice education of teachers. The programme will enable the teachers to use their academic freedom and autonomy collectively and in a more effective manner for the improvement of education.

As a further step in the same direction, the isolation of the school from the community must come to an end. For this purpose, we should develop programmes of mutual service and support between the school and the community. Similarly, the isolation of the education system from other social sub-systems (such as those of health, agriculture or industry) should also be done away with through appropriate linkages in general and vocational education.

Finance: The development of the educational programmes indicated in this study will certainly need a large investment of funds; and we have assumed that the total educational expenditure may be doubled over a period of ten years. This will be a big and difficult effort. But that is probably the minimum required.

Three important issues need to be highlighted In this respect. To begin with, it should be emphasized that, while educational development needs money, it cannot be achieved through money alone. The non-monetary inputs, such as good planning, creating a climate of hard work; or improving the commitment of teachers and motivation of students, are far more important. In fact, in most areas of education, we have now reached a point of large diminishing returns for further investment of funds; and it is only non-monetary inputs that can transform the situation. Secondly, the highest emphasis has to be laid on the more effective use of the existing investment in education, partly because additional funds will be difficult to come by, and mainly because there is so much waste and ineffectiveness in the existing system. Thirdly, we must make every effort to see that the unit costs go down without impairing quality (e.g., through modification of wage-structure, rational planning of institutions, adoption of larger pupil-teacher ratios where desireable, non-formal education, etc.). Otherwise we may never have the resources to provide good education to all our people.

Implementation

In the course of the earlier sections, we have put forward several major proposals. It is obvious that none of them is totally new and all that we can claim is to have made a selection of well-known recommendations built round the theme of the education of the common people and put them together in a coherent way, with some shifts in emphasis and a few modifications. The question to be answered, therefore, is this: Why is it that these recommendations were not implemented in the past and what strategy can we adopt to ensure a better implementation in the future? We should also admit that even these diagnostic and prescriptive questions are not new: they have been often asked in the past and also answered with equal frequency. We can, however, claim some novelty in the diagnosis we have offered and consequently in the remedial action we have proposed. In other words, our principal contribution is that we are suggesting a different and a new strategy of implementation.

Some wrong or inadequate answers: Strategies of implementation obviously depend upon our diagnosis of the failure to implement educational reforms in the past. It is, therefore, necessary to draw attention to some wrong diagnoses and wrong or inadequate answers that have been commonly given so far.

(1) It has been said that we are a nation of 'good planners and bad implementers'. It is true that we do specialise in talking about our good intensions and noble objectives. But our plans are certainly not flawless or even always good; and to say that we are bad implementers does not explain anything. We must still ask the further question: why and in what way are we bad implementers? Those who put forward the bad implementation theory generally assume that the bureaucracy is mainly, if not solely, responsible for implementation and blame it almost exclusively for the failure. This is neither fair nor correct. While no one denies that the bureaucracy has to bear considerable responsibility for our failure to implement educational plans, it is not the sole culprit. The responsibility to implement educational

plans rests on the society as a whole and not on any one of its sub-systems.

2) This game of trying to find a scapegoat for our failure to implement radical plans of educational reform does not end with the bureaucracy. Every agency concerned with educational development indulges in the game. For instance, the public at large very often blames the teachers who are supposed to have lost their commitment to learning and to the welfare of their students. Teachers do not take it lying down and blame the intelligent public for their indifference and the ignorant public for not appreciating the value(?) of the goods they sell, the politicians for all their unwarranted interference, the students for their indiscipline and lack of motivation, and the society itself for not giving them a better status and still better emoluments. The students, in turn, blame the teachers who are said to be often incompetent, dishonest, and liable to show caste prejudices, nepotism and favouritism, and the bureaucrats for their selfishness and corruption. The politicians themselves blame all others -the teachers, the students, the public, and the civil service. The Centre blames these States who blame the Centre; and so on. So the merry game goes round and round, each group or authority blaming every one except itself. In this drama full of dust and din, the only silent actor is the common man (the talisman suggested by Mahatma Gandhi) who bears the huge burden of educational costs without getting any education whatsoever. The fact of the matter is that each one of these agencies -the Central Government, States, public, teachers, students, administrators -has failed education and stands indicted unequivocally for not playing its due role. Every agency must, therefore, accept its share of the blame and make

amends. This alone will help us to solve the problem for which the search for scapegoats will not provide the answer.

3) Equally unsatisfactory are the pedagogic or technological solutions which, in our opinion, are only partial and at best, inadequate, answers. These include: better teachers (i.e., better general education, better professional training, better selection, and better emoluments); better curricular reform; better supervision; better administration; a greater use of the modern mass media; and for all these, more money. These are important issues and they have their own place in a total programme of educational reconstruction. But education cannot be equated with mere pedagogy. Its basic problems are rooted, not so much in pedagogy as in the interface between education and society, and not infrequently, in the society itself. There are no mere pedagogic solutions to these complex problems.

4) Yet another argument often put forward is that education does not receive adequate priority, that it is generally ranked below agriculture, power, industry, irrigation and family planning in most of our plan documents and that it is still regarded as 'social service' and not as 'investment'. These charges are only partially correct. Although plan outlays on education have been comparatively small and decreasing proportionately over the years, the total expenditure on education (Plan and non-Plan) is very high and, as pointed out earlier, second only to that on defence. It has also been increasing at about twice the rate of growth in GNP. In fact, it is possible to argue that we have given education a high priority as indicated by the very high level of total educational expenditures already reached, that the possibilities of further growth in educational

expenditures is limited and that such increases will have to face a serious competition from other developmental sectors and will have to be seriously weighed against alternative uses. Similarly, while we agree that educational expenditures should be looked upon as investment in man, we cannot really support larger expenditures on a mere linear expansion of the formal system of education which is so wasteful and inefficient and so skewed in favour of the haves. It is only a radical transformation of the system that can convert these expenditures into investment in the people of the country. Consequently, additional investments in education are justified only after such transformation has taken place or only to bring about such transformation.

5) Finally, the most common reason advanced for our failures is the lack of adequate resources. This of course is an argument that can be advanced for the failure of almost every development plan in a poor country; and we often indulge in the game of preparing costly plans of educational development and justifying or rationalising our failure or inaction on the ground that the needed funds are not available. In all such arguments based on the power of money, the usual assumption is that there are no problems which 'mere money' cannot solve. This is a fallacy. Some programmes in education (e.g., character-building) do not need money and we often fail because we use money to get what money can never buy. We also forget that the more relevant question in the present situation is, not what we can do if more resources are made available, but what we can do even within the existing resources. We also have little moral right to ask for more money when we waste such large resources inspite of our

poverty. We should also remember that, in poor nations, money will always be in short supply and that these nations will have to spend 'thought' and put in greater human effort to make up for inadequacies of monetary investment rather than the other way round. But we conveniently ignore this principle because it is always easier to spend money than thought (or to put in greater effort), especially if it is somebody else's money.

The Basic Issues. What then is the alternative diagnosis of We our failure to bring about a radical transformation in education? We have indicated our views on the basic causes of our failure, in their appropriate contexts, in the preceding discussion. But even at the risk of some repetition, it is essential to sum them up briefly. These include,

— the failure to transform the existing structure of formal education so as to make it elastic, dynamic, and supportive of the maximum possible freedom to schools, teachers and students to experiment and innovate;

— the failure to develop large-scale and effective programmes of nonformal education at all stages; neglect of micro-level living cells of education (i.e., the millions of learning groups where action and the reaction continually takes place between the teachers and learners or between the learners themselves), many of which have become diseased or even dead; failure to orient the educational system to the needs and interests of the common man and neglect of elementary and adult education; over-emphasis on secondary and higher education and on the educational needs and demands of the upper and middle classes; failure to take the hard decisions, both political and academic, without which a radical reform of secondary and higher education is not possible;

— failure to generate a strong and nation-wide movement for educational reform and to sustain it over the years, both within and without the educational system; and failure to develop the social and political forces that can help the people to come into their own; and failure to launch a programme of simultaneous and complementary social and educational transformation.

It is obvious that these are the basic issues involved; and unless adequate attention is given to them, it will not be possible to bring about the radical educational changes we need.

A New Approach

The new strategy of development based on an awareness of these fundamental causes of our failures in the past has several important aspects.

1) *Adequate and large-scale action:* To begin with, it is necessary to abandon our traditional approach to educational reform which is bureaucratic, selective and limited and to adopt a new approach based on the involvement of the people and a massive effort to meet the challenges facing us. In particular, we should not waste our time any longer in toying with essential and overdue reforms in the form of experimental or pilot projects. Instead, we should immediately launch carefully planned programmes on a scale proportional to the size and complexity of the problems that we desire to solve. For shaking up the system as a whole, we may have to mount a big national campaign or even adopt some drastic and unorthodox measures.

2) *Organisation of a popular movement:* Another important aspect of the strategy is, not to depend upon the State alone, but to organise a nation-wide intensive and popular movement to bring about the needed educational and social transformation. In the post-independence period, we have depended, almost exclusively, upon the State to bring about this transformation and the results have been far from happy. The experience of the past thirty years has shown that the State in India still represents, by and large, the haves and the upper and middle classes and that the, representatives of the weaker sections play only a minor role therein. This has naturally led to several distortions such as, emphasis on high-level trained manpower and bureaucracy rather than on the people themselves as the principal agents of change; catering to the needs and demands of the top 30 per cent of the people (which means giving more and better education to those who already have had some or a good deal) rather than to those of the bottom 30 per cent of the people (which means giving at least some education to those who have had none); stress on secondary and higher education rather than on adult and elementary education; resistance to all changes which would affect the privileged position of the upper and middle classes (e.g., the introduction of the common school) or reduction in the subsidies they now enjoy (such as increase in fees); and opposition to all reforms that would have affected the middle class value system on which the present system of education is based.

In a society like that of ours, the state has to intervene in favour of the poor and give them that essential support and protection which might enable them to overcome their basic handicap of poverty, at least partially. This is what Mahatma Gandhi meant by his talisman or the doctrine of Antyodaya. The state has failed to do so and has, on the whole, helped in passing on the benefits of the educational development to the upper and middle classes and to the rich and the well-to-do. It is, therefore, necessary to realise that we cannot leave the problem of radical educational reconstruction entirely to the sweet will of the state and that we must build up a nationwide popular movement in favour of these changes in order to compel the state to bring about the needed educational transformation. This is what we did not do in the past and this is the one major programme we should now take up. In other words, if we desire education for our people, there is no escape from organising the people to fight for it. This direct political mobilisation is essential for development in its true sense and without it, no radical transformation is possible, either in education or in society. It was the existence of this political mobilisation in the pre-independence period that created a climate in which both the educational and social systems functioned better; and it is the absence of a similar political mobilisation in the post-independence period that has led to a deterioration, both in education and society.

3) *A simultaneous struggle within and without the system:* Yet another major aspect of the new strategy of development is that we shall have to wage the war for the needed transformation, simultaneously within and without the educational system. There are some who argue that such a movement cannot be started within the educational system for a number of obvious reasons: the large size and inertia of the system; the class attitudes of the vast bulk of administrators, teachers and students who have

concentrated their attention or marginal changes in their own immediate interests rather than in favour of the ultimate good of the people; the rigidity of the system which does not permit innovation; the small number of committed individuals within the system to launch an effective struggle; and so on. We do not agree with this viewpoint which writes off the entire formal system of education and provides it with an alibi for total inaction. We hold the view that there are several good and committed individuals and many good elements within the system that must be roused and organised to build up an intensive movement within the educational system. But this task cannot be carried out or succeed unless we simultaneously organise a similar movement outside the system as well. During the past thirty years, we have concentrated, almost exclusively, on the reform of the system from within. This attempt has failed for obvious reasons. We cannot, therefore, leave educational reform to educational institutions, teachers and students alone, although they too have their own legitimate responsibilities and roles. Mahatama Gandhi had emphasised the need to work outside the educational system even with the ultimate objective of reforming the system itself. We must, therefore, organise a massive educational campaign outside the educational system with the help of competent and dedicated persons who do not belong to the system. The programmes of non-formal education provide a good basis for these efforts; and as shown earlier, excellent opportunities for the purpose are available at all stages, and especially in adult and elementary education. To the extent these outside efforts grow and succeed, the conditions within the system will also begin to change and it is this simultaneous action both within and without the educational system that will help us to bring about the essential educational transformation and provide good education to all the people.

4) *Primacy of work at the grass-roots level:* In the new strategy of development, there should be great emphasis at the micro-level, on the creation of living educational cells in the local communities. Work at this level, and particularly in rural areas, is extremely important. Every encouragement should be given to young and dedicated persons who are committed to this and propose to take up the programme as their life-mission. It is only when this work develops adequately that new ideas may be generated therein and rise to the top to give new directions to policy. Let us not forget that the educational revolution we need cannot begin in Delhi and spread to the villages. The probability that it may begin in villages and ultimately reach Delhi is far greater.

5) *Simultaneous struggle for social transformation:* The need to mount up a simultaneous programme of a complementary social transformation in support of this struggle for educational transformation has already been stressed. This is the most important aspect of the new strategy and the one basic condition for its success.

The change agents: If this new strategy is to grow and succeed, we cannot ignore the close relationship between education, social reform, and politics. We will have to mount up a major effort in three directions, the workers within the system will have to be made aware of the basic political issues involved in social and educational transformation and assisted. through proper organisation, to bring about the needed educational transformation; the social and constructive workers should be made aware of the political implications of their work and trained to use their programme for the ultimate objective of conscientising the people, giving them self-confidence, and helping them to assert themselves; and the political workers who do not realise the significance of the cultural and educational dimensions of political mobilisation should be made aware of them and should be helped to give due weight to them in all political programmes.

It is only such a three-fold, simultaneous, and coordinated effort that will help us to build a movement of adequate size, force, and dynamism to put across the significant programme for educational and social transformation visualised here.

Conditions essential for success: Before we conclude, we would like to emphasize that there is already a great awakening among the masses, an awakening which cannot be stifled and which it is in our national interest to promote. The educational transformation proposed here can be of great assistance in promoting this mass mobilisation; and this mass mobilisation itself can be a powerful instrument for their education and liberation.

The new strategy of development proposed in this study is based on the assumptions, that we accept the supremacy of the people; that we believe in a democratic, secular, and socialist society in which poverty and exploitation are eliminated by a modification of the social structure, an egalitarian wage-policy, curbs on the consumption of the well-to-do, guarantee of a minimum standard of living for all, and the widest possible opportunity to the citizens, irrespective of religion or social status, to participate in decision-making, in production, and in pursuit of knowledge and culture; and that we look upon education, along with direct political and moral action, as important instruments which can be used to support each other in bringing about this social transformation at an early date.

The success of these proposals will ultimately depend upon the number and quality of committed individuals who will share these views and are prepared to fight for them at all costs.

7

Social and Educational Transformation

Education cannot be considered in a vacuum. It is a subsystem of the society and is closely related to its cultural, economic, and political aspects. One can, therefore, talk meaningfully of education only against the background of (1) the diagnosis of the major weaknesses of the existing social order, (2) the concept of a desirable society, (3) the probable process of change from the existing to the desired social order, and (4) the role of education in bringing about this social transformation.

Indian Society

It is to be regretted that the national debate which Mahatma Gandhi initiated on the desirable society has been almost abandoned for the past several years and that it has not been possible to project a clear image of the society which we would like to create in our country. This is a task to which we should now address ourselves on a priority basis. But whatever the ideological or other differences on the subject, there seems to be unanimity on the view that the most objectionable aspects of our society are inequality and poverty. For centuries, the Indian society has been a dual, highly unequal society in which a few castes or classes at the top have wielded almost all the economic, political, and knowledge power, while the vast bulk of the people, who had no access to education and no part in political power, lived in great poverty, often at sub-human levels. During the past 175 years, several changes have taken place in the over-all social scene. The princes and zamindars have disappeared; but feudal values and life-styles still dominate the society in many ways, in both political and economic spheres. The base of the ruling groups has widened to include several middle castes as well as the rural elite.

The upper and middle classes, who, taken together, form the top 30 per cent of the income groups, wield most of the economic and political power and are also the principal beneficiaries of the modern system of education. At the same time, the poor people have increased considerably in absolute numbers and have been totally marginalised. They have little control over economic resources and large numbers of them live a life of drudgery and abject poverty. They have benefited only marginally from the formal system of education and still continue to be educated through the traditional forms of incidental and non-formal education which have been even more outmoded with the passage of time. In spite of adult franchise, they have little effective political power, partly because it is not supported by either economic or knowledge power, but mainly because they are fragmented and unorganised.

They thus mostly live in feudal, semi-feudal or primitive conditions, deprived of most good things of life. In spite of our acceptance of the goal of creating a new social order based on freedom, justice, equality, and the dignity of the individual, Indian society still continues to be highly stratified and unequal with a very wide gap separating the standards of living and life-styles of the few rich and well-to-do and the many who are poor and extremely poor. The most significant aspects of the social transformation we need will, therefore, include an egalitarian change wherein the vast masses of our people will be awakened and organised, will have a decent standard of living, will enjoy adequate political power, and participate effectively in decision making in all aspects of social and national life and will have the necessary facilities for their cultural and educational advancement. The most significant and essential step in securing this transformation is the awakening and organisation of the people; and whether this will or will not involve a violent upheaval will depend largely upon the attitude the 'haves' will adopt. If they try to impede the awakening and organisation of the people or to suppress it, violence would be inevitable. But it would be possible to avoid it if they can read the writing on the wall and adjust themselves gracefully to the inevitable.

Indian Education

India was, at one time, one of the most advanced countries of the world in education and made significant contributions to the development of man's knowledge and culture; and its seats of-learning or universities attracted scholars from far and wide. At the beginning of the nineteenth century when the foundations of the modern system of education began to the laid, this ancient glory had mostly vanished. But even the remnants of the traditional educational system as had then survived made it compare favourably with many contemporary nations of the world, although the situation can only be described as unsatisfactory by modern standards. At that time, the right to the highest education was the privilege only of the small upper crust of society, consisting invariably of the higher varnas. Instruction was imparted in a classical language which was not the language of the people and laid emphasis on religion and ritual. Even formal elementary education was considered to be necessary for boys belonging to the rich and well-to-do classes or the high castes only, and a very small proportion of girls and children of the common people had access to it. Moreover, education was meant only for children and youth and not for adults so that life-long education became the privilege of a microscopic minority.

It would have been in the larger interests of the country if the British administrators had built the new education system on the foundations of this traditional one. But they either ignored it or deliberately destroyed it and tried to create a new educational system, modelled after that in the U.K., with the objective of creating a class of educated persons who would know English, become familiar with Western knowledge through it, and act as interpreters and intermediaries between the rulers and the ruled. Incidentally, they also tried to spread education among girls and the common people, including the scheduled castes and scheduled tribes. But they consistently refused to accept responsibility for the education of the people on administrative and financial considerations, which, in their opinion, had 'decisive weight'.

They believed in the 'downward filtration theory' under which education and culture percolates inevitably from the classes to the masses. They, therefore, argued that they would only create an educated class in the first instance and that it would be the responsibility of this class, in due course, to educate the masses. They did realise this limited objective so that, when their rule came to an end in 1947, their main educational legary was the creation of the new system of formal education through which the upper and the middle classes benefited themselves. The poor people still remained outside the system: vast numbers of their children did not go to school; a large proportion of those enrolled dropped out very early; and the percentage of literacy was only about 14.

As a part of the struggle for political freedom, attempts were made between 1900 and 1947, to create a network of national schools and universities outside the formal education system which was controlled by the British Administration. But these remained very limited in scale. When education was transferred to Indian control in 1921, the Provincial Education Ministers, responsible to the legislatures with an elected majority, tried to promote programmes of adult and universal elementary education but could not achieve much, due largely to political and financial constraints. The main educational contribution of the educated classes in the pre-independence period was, therefore, to help themselves, i.e., they helped to spread secondary and higher education widely among the upper and middle classes through the private secondary schools and colleges which they organised, and they argued that once the impediment of British Rule was out of the way, they would take the earliest and the most effective steps to spread education among the people. That is why Gokhale observed that the educated people of this country would be on their trail when freedom would be won.

It is a pity that these promises to the people were mostly forgotten in the post-independence period and, instead of the most energetic drive for the education of the people which was expected, we had a large-scale linear expansion of the formal education system created by the British. It may be pointed out that we appointed a University Education Commission in 1948, a high-level Technical Man-power Committee in 1949, and a Secondary Education Commission in 1952. All these merely strengthened the British tradition of the education of the classes and over-emphasis on secondary and university education which now receive about 60 per cent of the total educational expenditure. On the other hand, no Elementary Education Commission has been appointed at all. It is true that Article 45 of the Constitution does lay down that the state shall 'strive' to provide, by 1960, compulsory and free education for all children till they reach the age of 14 years. But this provision has no effective sanction and has not been implemented even to this date. Adult education has been almost totally ignored and receives less than one per cent of the total educational outlay. Even the hope that the institutions of national education would blaze out a new trial has been destroyed because they were soon coopted within the formal education system which is now a gigantic structure with about 700,000 educational institutions, 100 million students, more than 3.5 million teachers, and an expenditure of about Rs.25,000 million which is next only to that on defence. In spite of all this expansion and all the changes made therein, however, the educational system still continues to benefit mainly the upper and middle classes for whom it was originally designed. It still makes only a marginal contribution to the education of the people, and especially of the poor people, who have only a limited access to it, both qualitatively and quantitatively. In fact, the total injustice of the system and its unpardonable discrimination against the poor can be highlighted by the following indisputable facts:

1. About 60 per cent of the people (age 10 and over) are still illiterate and have received none of the benefits of this vast educational system.

2. About 20 per cent of the children, mostly the lowest of the low, never enter the schools at all. They are born poor and continue to be poor and the formal system of education bypasses them altogether.

3. Of those children that enter the schools, nearly half drop out by class V and nearly three-fourths drop out by class VIII; only about 15 per cent reaches class XII, and less than one per cent get the first degree.
4. As pointed out above, the system accords very low priority to programmes such as adult education, universal elementary education, or non-formal education which would benefit the masses especially the poor. On the other hand, it accords high priority and invests the bulk of its resources in secondary and higher education which benefit mostly the top 30 per cent of the population.
5. The children from poor families generally get an unfair deal in the system whose entire ethos is oriented to the needs and aspirations of the upper and middle classes and which still continues to use English as the medium of instruction in higher education and thereby encourages the use of English as a medium at the school stage also.

It would, therefore, be incorrect to describe the existing educational system as an instrument for educating the people; the evidence adduced above clearly shows that it is more appropriately designed for not educating them. In fact, the primary objective of the system is not to spread education among the people, but to function as an efficient and merciless mechanism to select individuals who should continue to remain in the privileged sector or enter it afresh. It does not discharge even this task impartially and, as we shall see presently, functions in such a biased fashion that those who are already in the priviledged sector find it easier to continue therein while the underprivileged find that the access to the privileged sector through the portals of education is becoming more restricted and increasingly dependent on chance rather than on merit. The main achievement of the system, therefore, is to condemn the bulk of the children of the common people as drop-outs and failures and to consign them to a life of drudgery and poverty which has hardly any parallel in the contemporary world or even in our own earlier history.

This neglect of the people of India, in whom the Constitution vests the ultimate sovereign authority, is harmful, not only to the common man, but also to the health and development of the nation as a whole. As native talent is randomly distributed among the people, we have one-seventh of the potential talent of the world; and yet our achievements in every sphere are negligible for the simple reasons that a vast reservoir of our talent remains unidentified and uncultivated. This jeopardises the future of the entire country and eventually of the upper and middle classes as well. Even from the point of view of narrow self-interest, therefore, the ruling groups must realise that they are harming themselves and the ultimate development of the country itself by keeping the common man of India continually deprived of education and other good things of life.

Education and Society

It will thus be seen that our educational and social systems reinforce one another: both are highly unjust and inegalitarian; the beneficiaries of both are the upper and middle classes; and both marginalise the common people. What is worse, the inherent tendency of our system of formal education (on which we place an almost exclusive emphasis) is to continue the status quo and perpetuate the wide differences between the rich and well-to-do on the one hand and the poor people on the other. As is well known, our educational system has a small group of good quality and prestigious schools (including the public and English-medium schools) which are availed of by the rich and well-to-do and a large number of government and other publicly maintained schools whose standards are unsatisfactory and which are mostly used by the poor people. The children of the rich and well-to-do classes, therefore, get into the good quality schools and later come to hold important and prestigious positions in life for which the schools qualify them. On the other hand, a significant proportion of the children of the poor people do not enter the school system at all, or get into the poor quality schools, drop out sooner rather than later, and excepting for a few who get into the privileged sector, generally get back into the same underprivileged social groups to which they originally belonged. Besides, the children from the well-to-do classes who enter the system earlier study under better conditions and stay longer, get an essential superiority over the children from the poor social groups who have none of these advantages, and find it comparatively easy to continue in the privileged group. Even if a child from the poorer social groups has the same attainments as that of a child from the privileged groups (and this really involves a much larger effort), he is still at a disadvantage vis-a-vis his well-to-do rival in a society where 'who knows who' is so important. The net result of all these factors is that, our inegalitarian and hierarchical educational system leads to an inegalitarian and hierarchical social system, just as the inegalitarian educational system arose, in the first instance, from the inegalitarian social system itself.

This does not mean that there are no forces for change in the system. In fact, there is an under-current of egalitarian change, in both education and society, which reflects itself through such programmes as universalisation of elementary education, provision of scholarships to talented but economically handicapped children, special effort for the spread of education among girls or schemes of special assistance for scheduled castes and tribes. Unfortunately, slogans have been more forceful than action in these important programmes so that all that we have been able to achieve is to provide some vertical mobility to a fortunate few among the deprived groups. But such individuals are readily coopted within the system which merely helps to legitimise it, in spite of all its grave injustices to the common man.

What is the precise relationship between educational and social transformation? The most commonly accepted view romanticises this relationship and argues that we must begin with a radical transformation in education which, in its turn, will bring about a radical transformation in society. On the other hand, there is also a view that the social structure will always be reflected within the education system which it dominates so that no worthwhile educational reform is possible unless a social revolution is first brought about. The truth is probably neither so simple nor so direct.

The educational system has a duty to make a critical analysis of the social system, to focus attention as its internal contradiction and on the gap between slogans and practice, and to highlight the need for structural changes, where necessary, including those needed within the educational system itself. Education can thus play a useful role in promoting the desire for a radical social change and also help in deciding the nature of such change as well as the manner of bringing it about. Similarly, education is essential to complete and consolidate a social change decided and implemented through political means, whether by bullets or by the ballot.

The education system can also remedy social deficiencies which are due to educational factors. But it can have little effect on social deficiencies which arise elsewhere, say, in the economic or political sub-systems. We must also remember that, while it is comparatively easy to introduce educational reforms that support the existing social structure, it is extremely difficult, if not impossible, to implement radical educational reforms which threaten the existing social structure or run counter to its imperatives. All things considered, it appears that, if we desire to get out of this vicious circle wherein an inegalitarian society creates an inegalitarian educational system and vice versa, we must mount a big offensive on both social and educational fronts.

The major implications of this proposal, for both social and educational reforms, can be briefly indicated.

(1) In society, the basic minimum change required is to narrow down the existing wide gap between the life-styles and standards of living of the upper and middle classes and the common people by,

- — eliminating or at least minimising all direct and indirect forms of exploitation;
- — imposing limits and curbs on the consumption of the rich and the well-to-do through a modification of the existing arbitrary and inegalitarian wage-structure and other allied measures;

Ensuring a basic minimum standard of living to the people through (a) an emphasis on increased production of goods and services needed by the common man, (b) a guarantee of employment at a reasonable wage to all able-bodied persons who are willing to work, and (c) the organisation of an efficient and nation-wide public distribution system of food-stuffs and other essential commodities.

An important implication of this policy will be to reduce the wide gulf between urban and rural areas and to improve the standards of living of the rural people, especially of agricultural labour and small and marginal farmers.

(2) In education, the corresponding basic minimum change required is to make the common people, rather than the upper and middle classes, the principal beneficiaries of the educational system. This will imply, among other things, giving the highest priority to the programmes for the education of the common people such as adult education including liquidation of illiteracy, non-formal education of out-of-school youth, and universal elementary education including the adoption of the common school system;

— utilising the bulk of additional resources available on programmes for the education of the people so that they, and not secondary and higher education, receive the larger share of total educational expenditure;

— changing the basic values underlying the system and orienting them to the common people instead of to the upper and middle classes;

— adopting the regional languages as media of instruction at all stages;

— transforming the content of education to suit the ethos of work and production and the imperatives of national development; improving the access of students from economically handicapped groups to secondary and higher education-and taking suitable measures for optimising their performance;

— eliminating or reducing the subsidies in secondary and higher education that now go to the upper and middle classes; increasing financial support to the deserving students from deprived social groups; and

— restructuring educational administration on the basis of decentralisation of decision-making authority so that the common people are actively involved in planning and implementation of their own educational programmes.

Major reason for our failure to bring about a radical reconstruction of the educational system in the past has been the fact that we have ignored the close relationship between social and educational transformation and the consequent need for a simultaneous effort on both the fronts. The most significant aspect of our future strategy of educational development should, therefore, be to plan and implement a radical, simultaneous and complementary programme of social and educational reform.

New Concept and Structure of Education

A detailed discussion of the social transformation to be attempted as a part of this package deal of simultaneous social and educational transformation is outside the scope of this exercise which concentrates on the educational transformation we need. The central programme of this transformation is a radical reform of the value system, processes, and organisation of the formal system of education which we have laboured over 150 years to create and which has now become a gigantic enterprise which mostly keeps the poor people out does not even provide good education to the bulk of its students, and also hinders the social transformation we seek. The task is of the highest priority; and any delay in its implementation implies that the size of the formal system and its inertia will increase further in the meantime and that this will add to the cost and energy required to reform it

Value System

The existing educational system lays greater emphasis on individualism, competition, verbal fluency or linguistic ability, and mere acquisition of information. What is even worse, the ethos of the existing -system is highly authoritarian where values such as equality, love of truth, or spirit of enquiry cannot be fostered. In the new concept of education, we should recognise the significance of social objectives, cooperation and team-work, the complementarity of intellectual and manual work, promotion of skills, and the building up of character. Similarly, great emphasis will have to be placed on promoting a scientific outlook on life and the basic values of pursuit of truth, equality, freedom, justice and dignity of the individual.

An Integrated, Participatory System of Formal and NonFormal Education

The existing system places an almost exclusive emphasis on formal education and on teaching instead of on learning. In the new system, emphasis will have to be shifted from teaching to learning and incidental and non-formal education should receive an equal. If not even greater emphasis, and the formal, incidental, and non-formal systems should be blended together in an integrated fashion. In the existing system, there is only one channel of full-time attendance. In the new system, all the three channels of full-time, part-time, and own-time education should be freely used and should have equal status so that it would be possible for a student to transfer himself from one to the other according to his needs. The existing system operates on the basis of a single-point entry, sequential annual promotions, and an almost unbroken. continuous stretch of education. In the new system, recurrent education should be developed and promoted; and there should be several points of entry as well as flexibility for condensing or prolonging the duration of courses of levels. It would, therefore, be possible for a student to join and step off the education system whenever and as often as may be necessary, and also to regulate the pace of his studies. The existing system places an almost exclusive emphasis on full-time professional teachers and on the school as the sole educational institution. In the new system, all teaching resources available in the community should be utilised and all social institutions should be used for educational purposes. In fact. the new educational system should be extremely flexible to meet the needs of life-long learning for every individual. It should also allow for the fullest participation by institutions and individuals ordinarily considered to be outside the educational system and also mere towards abolishing the distinction between teachers (who are really senior students) and students (who in effect are junior teachers) because every individual should be learning whatever he is interested in from others and simultaneously teaching whatever he can to those who are interested to learn it from him. In fact, the new educational system may rightly be described as education of the people, for the people, and by the people.

Relevance and Transformation of Content: A major weakness of the existing system is the lack of relevance of most of what we teach, not only to the poor people who are outside the system, but even to the upper and middle classes who are inside it. This irrelevance arises from several factors such as,

— an over-emphasis on mere acquisition of information;

— the common practice of framing curricula with an ascending objective, viz., the curriculum of the elementary school prepares a student for the secondary stage, the secondary school fits a student for a college and almost unfits him for everything else, and a B.A. degree tries to make a person eligible for a master's degree or a well-paid and generally white-collar job. Such curricula obviously become irrelevant to those who do not proceed to the next stage and these generally constitute the vast majority) or fail to get a job; the organisation of the curriculum mainly on the basis of middle-class values which cannot be generalised and which have no relevance to the life and needs of the vast majority of the people; the practice of centralised curriculum construction and the great emphasis placed on uniformity rather than on diversity which makes it difficult, if not impossible, to relate education to local environment or to individual aptitudes and capacities; and the failure to adjust the content of education to changing social or national needs, due mainly to the inertia of the system.

This irrelevance of education progressively alienates the intellectual community from the people and the basic problems of the society. It is, therefore, obviously necessary to take appropriate steps to remove these causes that lead to irrelevance in the content of education. But this is not enough; and we must also adopt a number of positive measures to make the content of education relevant to social transformation and national development. Among these, the following deserve emphasis:

(1) The cultural aspects of education which are generally neglected at present should receive considerable emphasis. Students should be helped to 'discover' India, to be patriotic, to take a proper pride in their cultural heritage, and yet to be sensitive to modern ideas and values and to the

weaknesses in our own tradition which have to be overcome.

(2) Mahatma Gandhi had rightly diagnosed that the traditional middle class values of glorifying intellectual work and denigrating manual labour (which had dominated our educational system and led to a total divorce between work and education) had disastrous effects, on both the individual and the society. What a healthy, egalitarian, and non-exploitative society needed was a citizen who was a good productive worker as well as an educated and cultured individual. He, therefore, advocated the view that good education must reunite work and education. This would make the upper and middle classes better individuals because participation in socially useful productive work, not only develops skills, but cultivates the intellect and values as well.

It will also enrich the masses who would receive education and be able to resist exploitation through organised effort.

(3) In a poor society like that of ours, development is so significant and urgent that, over the next 10-15 years we must make every person development-minded and induce him to work intensively for it on the basis of the highest priority. Such a national objective cannot be realised if the education system which, as pointed out earlier, now involves about 16 per cent of the entire population and consumes nearly four per cent of the national income were to be neutral to this developmental effort or, as often happens, pursues even contrary objectives. We just cannot afford to run education and development as two separate and parallel (or even partially contradictory) systems. It would be far more effective and economical to run them as complementary systems, each supporting the other.

This can happen only if development, like work, also becomes a medium of education and all students and teachers are involved in appropriate programmes of development at all stages of education.

(4) The proper teaching of science and an appropriate technology must be emphasized at all stages of education. Science can be of great help to rid our traditional society of superstition, fatalism, and irrational fear and in promoting the rational temper which a modern society needs. Appropriate technology can help us to abolish poverty and ill-health and to raise the standards of living of the people. Every citizen must, therefore, be aware of the potential of science and technology and adequate competence to use them.

(5) Great emphasis is to be laid on the ethos necessary for the democratic, socialist, and secular society we desire to create. Negatively, it implies a fight against traditional values and customs which impede the creation of this new society, e.g., casteism, communalism, inequality of men and women, of feudal and capitalist life-styles. Positively, it implies the development of such values and skills as tolerance, self-restraints, concern for others, commitment to basic human values and a capacity to fight and suffer for them if necessary, ability to work together with other individuals and groups in shared programmes with common objectives, and willingness and capacity to resolve conflicts through discussion, give and take and other peaceful means.

Standards. Education is a double-edged tool. If it is of good quality, it helps individual growth, social transformation, and national development. But if proper standards are not maintained, it can lead both individuals and societies down the hill to personal disaster or social disintegration. Maintaining the quality of education thus becomes a task of supreme importance. Relevance of content is an important but only one aspect of the problem, The second is the provision of adequate facilities -institutions, teachers, equipment. The third is the creation of a climate of hard, sustained, and dedicated work by teachers and students because education is essentially a stretching process. It should be emphasized, however, that standards should not be measured, as at present, merely by the extent of information acquired by the students or by their linguistic ability, especially in English. They should be measured in broader individual and social terms by the total personality development of the students and by the social commitments and contributions of students, teachers, and educational institutions.

In the existing educational system, the standards of education maintained are good in a small number of institutions which, as pointed out earlier, are used by the small upper crust of rich and well-to-do persons. On the other hand, the standards are poor or even deplorable in the vast majority of the institutions which are used by the bulk of the people. In the new system of education, there is no place for this dualism. This does not, however, mean an indiscriminate equalisation of all institutions. In secondary and higher education, in particular, there would no doubt be some high quality and pace-setting institutions in every sector. But the position would differ from the present one in two significant ways. On the one hand, access to these high quality institutions would not be confined to the privileged as at present, and effort would be made to ensure that, through a well-planned programme of cultivation of talent, scholarships and placement, these institutions would also be availed of by talented children from the under-privileged social groups. On the other hand, the standards in the bulk of the institutions which are very unsatisfactory at present would be substantially raised and no institution would be allowed to fall below certain prescribed levels.

Flexibility, Diversity, and Dynamism

The present educational system is based on an over-emphasis on centralisation and uniformity and has consequently become rigid and inelastic: the axiom that either all move or none moves can only make everyone immobile. In a vast and plural society like that of ours, the attempts to create a uniform and rigid educational system is foredoomed to failure. It will also be counter-productive because every such attempt will fall below the capacity of good schools which will not be able to utilise their full potential just as it will be beyond the reach of the weaker institutions and lead to still greater inefficiency. India stands for unity in diversity. We should, therefore, try to evolve a unity in the fundamentals at the national level and then evolve a highly decentralised, flexible, and dynamic system which provides adequate scope for diversity, experimentation and innovation by state systems, schools, and teachers.

8

Mobilisation, People's Participation and Decentralisation

A New Commitment to Human Development

Through several landmark events since the turn of the decade, commitment has been made at the highest level to improve the living conditions and future of millions: the World Conference on Education for All in Jomtien, Thailand in March 1990 launched a worldwide initiative to meet basic learning needs. Countries pledged to meet the goal of education for all by the year 2000 and the achievement of a functional and sustainable level of learning and life skills by at least 80 per cent of their youth. The Convention on the Rights of the Child, that made free and compulsory primary education an obligation of the state and the right of all children, came into effect in September 1990. Since then, over 150 countries have ratified the Convention, beating the record of any other human rights treaty. The World Summit for Children, the first truly global summit ever held, established a range of social development goals, including universal access to primary education and completion of the primary cycle by at least 80 per cent of those enrolled. Upon receiving their joint Nobel Peace Prize in November 1993, ANC leader Nelson Mandela and President Frederick de Klerk of South Africa pledged to make these goals national priorities.

Beyond the issue of human dignity, some common strands tie these various global meetings together. Firstly, the recognition that people are the end purpose and the principal means of development. "A one hundred year programme must be based on the development of education," says a Chinese proverb, reflecting education's strategic position in a country's progress. Research has demonstrated that higher per capita income levels go hand in hand with higher literacy levels. Similarly, numerous studies conducted around the world underline the linkages between female education, reduced fertility and increased economic productivity, thereby providing a key to slowing down population growth.

Secondly, participation, in its various dimensions, has become recognised as a basic principle of action, an overall development strategy. In the context of basic education, participation implies engaging people, including parents, children, teachers, political authorities and business leaders, widely and actively in defining learning needs, running the school and enhancing resources for education. Such a participatory culture can only grow and be sustained in an environment which genuinely recognises its value. It requires certain structures, and cannot be applied in the sphere of education alone.

Thirdly, there is a realisation that beyond high-level political commitment, the goals set at these various summits cannot be achieved without a strong degree of social mobilisation, meaning people's participation through organised and systematic actions. In the context of basic education, mobilisation refers to the active involvement of all relevant sectors of society in promoting and supporting education. As the UNICEF background paper underlines, the martial overtone of the term is not accidental. It reflects a sense of urgency about overcoming a common problem or achieving a common purpose through expression of a society's collective commitment, formulation of strategies to achieve results, and engagement of large numbers of people in coordinated and goaloriented group actions. Social mobilisation for education has often taken the form of one-shot, short-term campaigns, around a particular action or goal. While it has been given greater attention in literacy, adult education and the nonformal education spheres, less common are social mobilisation efforts in the context of the regular school system and the basic learning needs of children. This is beginning to change, a process highlighted in the ways countries prepared their EFA national action plans, through consulting a broad spectrum of political and educational interests, including sectors traditionally marginalised from the educational discussion.

Fourthly, community participation is perceived as a necessity from a financial point of view, since developing countries cannot finance education adequately without a large measure of support from the community. In China, the giant of the nine countries with a population of 1.2 billion, $12 billion is allocated annually to educate 180 million students. As a comparison, the United States spends $440 billion on 40 million children. Lastly, community participation is vital to ensuring sustainability.

Unless a community, starting with parents, can grasp the short and long-term benefits of the educational cause, it will be very difficult, if not impossible, to make the school a true centre for living and learning.

Democratising Governance for Greater Participation

In order for people to participate at the local level,

structures of governance have to become more flexible and responsive to local needs. In many countries, the trend toward democratisation has been accompanied by a gradual decentralisation of power from the central government and capital city to regions, districts, towns and villages.

Various forms of decentralisation -deconcentration, delegation and devolution of authority and functions - have been introduced or are being debated in most developing countries. Although evidence shows that decentralisation has often led to the expansion of basic education opportunities, in other cases it has had a negative effect on equity, quality anti social cohesion.

Today, this momentum of participation, mobilisation and action at global, national and community levels has to be maintained and strengthened. Furthermore, it can be nourished by the success of past endeavours, such as the Green Revolution, in which social mobilisation played a decisive role. More recently, the global child immunisation campaign, touted as the largest collective peacetime effort in world history, could not have been achieved without engaging large numbers of people, from parents and village leaders to heads of state.

Arguably, the task is more difficult in the educational field, since it requires a longer-term and firmer commitment on the part of families, children and political leaders. But success stories in other fields contain lessons and clues that are potentially valuable to the promotion of EFA, especially universal primary education. Seeking to distill these lessons, the UNICEF presentation distinguishes eight major components of what needs to be done to maximise the impact of social mobilisation. To various degrees and according to their needs, the nine high-population-countries have pegged their EFA strategies to these guidelines.

Key Elements of a Strategy to Expand Social Mobilisation

1. A clearly articulated goal and vision

For effective mobilisation 10 Occur, people need to feel they are working toward a defined goal. The internationally adopted target of access to primary education in a formal or an equivalent programme for all children by the year 2000, with at least 80 per cent of them completing the primary stage, provides an easily and widely understood focus for advocacy, participation, mobilisation, programme planning anti monitoring. The class of 2000, consisting of all current primary entry-age children, deserves everything their societies can give them to ensure a successful outcome by this date. Providing them with the support they need to stay in school and learn what they need to learn should become the pivot of a nationwide mobilisation in each country.

2. High profile and frequent monitoring

An education programme of universal scope that aims to reach large numbers within a specific time-table must develop an effective method of monitoring progress. National leaders at the highest level can use the monitoring system as an effective instrument for mobilisation and action by personally leading public reviews of progress, deciding on remedial actions and encouraging officials down the line to do the same.

3. Visibility on the national agenda

If the, whole of society is expected to participate in and mobilise around universal primary education, it must be, brought to the centre of national attention. It must be shown how primary education provides benefits across the board, such as better health, labour productivity, greater democratic participation, and slowing of population growth. National leaders have to take the lead in this nationwide dialogue in order to build public awareness and understanding leading to support and involvement of the whole society.

4. Building a national consensus

Participation and mobilisation on an enduring basis can only be promoted on the foundation of a national consensus on the major goals and priorities, and the main strategies for achieving them. Consensusbuilding is an ongoing process that needs to be nurtured. Consensus on basic goals and strategies must be non-partisan enough to survive change of government and personalities in high places.

5. Identifying, emulating and creating success stories

It is essential to identify promising examples of success - creative and innovative combinations of action that have injected fresh blood into systems and accelerated progress. All of the nine countries have examples of success which need to he studied and adapted for wider application.

6. Decentralisation based on shared responsibilities

Decentralisation of responsibility and functions must be introduced and implemented in such a way that it is not seen as an excuse for abdicating the state's responsibility for basic education or as a means of shifting the burden from the central authorities to the local level. Decentralisation works when it is a means of redistributing functions and authority among different levels of Government and of the civil society in order to make, systems more efficient and democratic, allowing people to Participate and contribute. It must also hold them accountable: one of the major reasons for the success of the immunisation campaign lay in the number of people held responsible in the effort. In India for example, every district chief, every governor was held accountable for achieving a goal. Chief ministers in states, falling short of targets received personal letters from the late prime minister, Rajiv Gandhi.

7. Building on existing institutions and practices

The starting point for promoting popular participation, social mobilisation and decentralisation have to be the existing institutions, practices and norms in each society. Local goverment in one form or another has always existed. There are traditional structures for community efforts, as well as religious, cultural, labour, professional and other types of organisations and collective entities. It is important to identify the potential and shortcomings of these institutions and practices, build on their strengths and devise ways of overcoming their weaknesses.

8. Effective use of modern communication

"This is the most revolutionary tool that we have. The use of radio, television, videocassettes and tapes provides ways of motivating and energising populations that never existed thirty years ago," says UNICEF's Executive Director, James P. Grant. Yet, the potential of the communication media for expanding people's access to educational opportunities and for mobilising people's support for and involvement in education is far from being fully exploited.

Top-level Commitment to Participation

Over the past decades, educational systems have moved in the direction of greater adherence to participatory norms, more effective social mobilisation and increased decentralisation of authority and responsibility, but much still needs to be done to bridge the gap between theory and practice. These interrelated and overlapping concepts are guiding forces behind individual countries' Education for All action plans. In many cases, they have been enshrined constitutionally. In Indonesia, the 1989 Education Law states that education is the responsibility of the state, the community, and the family. In China, the 1985 "Decision on Reform of China's Educational Structure" granted decision-making powers for administration of primary education to local authorities. The 1992 Amendments to the Indian Constitution opened a new chapter in the process of democratic decentralisation in India by making it mandatory for all States and Union Territories to establish regular democratically elected bodies for local self-government. "It is a very major step in strengthening our concept of decentralisation and giving power and authority to the village bodies," said Ram Niwas Mirdha, an Indian member of parliament. There is provision for a state finance commission to decide upon resource allocation from the state to the village level.

Often, these measures give official sanction to long-held traditions. Community participation in Indonesian education can be traced back to national movements, such as the Taman Siswa (The Garden of Students) in the early 1920s that was based on the conviction that Indonesia could not achieve independence and prosperity unless its people were educated. Indonesia also harbours a core of traditional values, such as arriving at a consensus and assisting the needs of fellow community members which have been influential in shaping national identity. In India, the system of local

government known as Panchayati Raj has functioned in varying forms for centuries. The Latin American movement of Educacion Popular has a historic and well-entrenched stronghold in Brazil, especially rooted in the NGO sector. In China, community-run schools as well as community-paid teachers have played a crucial role in the overall expansion of basic education: about 40 per cent of the teachers in primary schools are paid by the community.

Many educational programmes in the nine most populous countries emphasise community participation: in Nigeria, where the adult literacy rate is just over 50 per cent, a National Mass Literacy Campaign was launched by the government in 1992, under the slogan "Each One Teach One or Fund the Teaching of One." The strategy is aimed at encouraging every literate person in the country to be part of the effort to educate the illiterate population. In China, community support and participation in improving classrooms have contributed significantly to increased floor space per pupil in primary schools. In India, the National Literacy Mission has worked best where there has been a high degree of social participation, involving the forging of a broad-based alliance between the district administration, NGOs and social activists.

As several delegations underlined however, participation does not spring up automatically. How can rural, illiterate parents for instance, be expected to participate? Over and above the important issue of inadequate remuneration, why should teachers embrace new teaching methods and increased community participation? For people to feel the impetus to participate, a participatory culture has to be nurtured. It has to overcome obstacles like rigid legal systems, bureaucratic institutions and attitudes, entrenched political interests, and inequities in the distribution of wealth and power. "There has to be a mobilising force," said Malini Bhattachavya, a member of Parliament from West Bengal, emphasizing the importance of partnerships. "In our case, we have found that the literacy programme has been most successful in places where local administration, local parties, political actors at the grassroots level and NGOs have acted as a mobilising agency."

Motivating Communities and Families

The full benefits of participation cannot be reaped without forming partnerships at the local, state and national levels. Who are the key actors in spreading and sustaining quality education? Firstly, the parents, and mothers in particular. Women are the first and most important promoters of children's education. Their expectations and attitudes towards their children's schooling are an important factor in learning achievement. Research in several countries shows that schools which attain a high level of quality generally also enjoy a strong degree of parental support. Lending this support demands a long-term commitment that can range from five years to more than a decade. Parents must feel that there are clear economic and Social benefits in schooling their children, especially their girls. "Such benefits are possible if the education is high quality, based on modern science and technology, and linked to the national development programme," Said Fay Chung chief of UCEF's Education Cluster. It takes enlightened leadership to convince families -especially ones with working children of the value of education. In Bangladesh, mothers' groups have been organised locally in different parts of the country. In many rural areas, "Mothers' Rallies" have been successfully organised resulting in substantial improvements in school enrolment, attendance and retention.

Such efforts are indispensable to foster motivation at the community level and raise awareness toward the importance of basic education. "We all presume that there is a great desire and rush for joining school and the educational system. It is not so," said Ram Niwas Mirdha.

"You have to motivate Parents that education will bring their family, their children, their boys, their girls the benefits that they desire." In his intervention, Mr. Mirdha noted that in many villages, even people who had been to School feel disillusioned with education, partly because it had not led to regular paid jobs. Two observations Stem from this: firstly the real purpose of education needs to be better defined: "We should clearly say that it is not for jobs that we are giving education, but for providing you better tools for improving your lives and your situation," said Mirdha. "If you are a carpenter, you will be a better carpenter. If you are an agriculturist, you will be a better agriculturist with education." Secondly, The relevance of the curriculum to the lives of village boys and girls deserves close attention.

Making Learning More Relevant

The inherently conservative nature of the classroom was underlined by panelists and speakers front the floor, bringing the critical question of quality to the forefront of discussion the image of the classroom is still closely Linked to the school house, the teacher, chalk, blackboard and notebook. "There's no other field of major human endeavour where the primary thrust is still so closely linked to patterns of one hundred years ago," said UNICEF's Executive Director. This traditionalism permeates the entrant and methodology of the school curriculum. More often than not, parents remain outsiders to the school system, students are passive listeners in the classroom and teachers are passive executors of predetermined curricula. "Such Schools are unable to cope with changes in the modern world, or to adapt learning to the cultural and social realities faced by their pupils and parents," said Fay Chung. "The school of today must overcome these developmental problems both in terms of relevance to the community and in terms of establishing a curriculum which is both universal and yet specifically tailor-made for a particular culture and situation."

In this endeavour participation also plays a key role. "If High quality and relevance be achieved without the marriage of the highest level academic and professional knowledge and skills with the interests, preoccupations and commitment of the ordinary community," Ms Chung explained. This requires striking a balance between the national and local levels, and distinguishing in what areas the various partners in education can most usefully participate and contribute. Developing the curriculum should not only involve the best available Specialists, but also the supervisors, teachers and trainers, with inputs from industry, religious interests, and parents where appropriate. Such was the format adopted in Egypt in February 1993: a conference for developing primary education curricula brought together representatives from different parties, intellectuals and cultural leaders, business representatives, parents, teachers, religious leaders, ministry personnel and international experts. The conference represented an attempt to provide a channel for public input and furnished an example of public participation in the decision-making and priority-setting process.

In this style of endeavour, the end goal is to unite the universal to the specific in both national and local terms, so that national development is not divorced from specific histories and cultures. Again, the imperative of a united vision based on relevance and quality is reiterated. Without the required technical capacity and social sensitivity, locally designed curricula and textbooks may be even more rigid and prescriptive than those produced centrally. They may also be weak pedagogically and lack creativity. The concept of a core curriculum with options that can be changed by communities is a useful one.

"There is no need to see only one school type as the answer," affirmed Ms Chung. "It is possible to have a dozen school types. It is possible to marry the formal and the informal approaches. It is essential to have different types of schools for different clienteles."

Some of the most successful educational programmes are ones that are linked to poverty alleviation schemes, and include health services and improved nutrition. In China, for example, local authorities in rural areas have taken an integrated approach toward educational development, combining it with local development plans, namely through technical and vocational training As a result, "the cultural and technical quality of the rural workforce has risen considerably, agricultural production has been boosted and the rural inhabitant's living standards have been improved," said Mr Liu-Bin, vice-chairman of the Chinese State Education Commission. "Facts have proven that this sytem is conducive to combining educational development with the peasant's wish to boost agricultural production." Some 600,000 school factories and enterprises have also been created, adding income to public resources. In Brazil, municipalities have been behind successful experiences to provide access to basic education in dis-advantaged areas of the northeast. hi Jaguare-Espirito Santo, rural schools were created to prevent migration to urban centers, with the option of part-time attendance allowing children to work during the harvest season. In far-flung corners of the country, special emphasis has been given to distance teaching and the training of teachers.

It follows that the involvement of' the community in implementing the curriculum and running the schools is equally important. Here, the potential contribution of every sector needs to be scrutinised. "The school and community must reinforce one another," said Ms Chung.

"The school must be seen as an important and valuable asset belonging to the community." Participation from the local community can provide valuable extra resources. It can take the form of helping construct new buildings, renovating old ones, and raising funds for extra teaching materials. Local communities should have a say in the appointment of teachers and on timetables. Although the training and monitoring of teachers is best done at the national level the resources of paraprofessionals, whom Ms Chung compares to "barefoot doctors", cannot be underestimated. When the government of Zimbabwe was involved in setting up schools in camps for Mozambican refugees, teachers were recruited from the camp. Many had no more than a grade four education at best. Ten years later, these people have become fully trained teachers with nine years of education. Dr. Mahbub ul Haq underlined the necessity for audacious teacher recruiting measures to fill the need for 1.6 million additional teachers in the next seven years. He suggested that some countries consider, for example, drafting university students to work as primary school teachers for it part of their course.

Co-operation with NGOs, the Private Sector anu the Media

Governments also have a valuable partner in NGOs. In the field of education, many have developed innovative programmes adapted to local needs that have reached and empowered the poorest groups. Their links with local networks provide them with unique sources of information and authority. Bangladesh is a pioneer in the NGO sector. Using the Simplest buildings and training village women as teachers, BRAC and other voluntary agencies can provide primary schooling at about one-third the cost of formal schooling through government. In Pakistan, the government's Social Action Programme emphasizes the role of NGOs, although comprehensive research still needs to be undertaken in order to assess the various initiatives and lessons learned from NGO experiences. Many operate schools in homes, improvised premises and self-constructed schools, using para-professional teachers, but such initiatives are not always matched by innovative or non-traditional teaching methods. Again, this fact underlines the need for clearly defined national standards that are a yardstick for measuring quality.

Secondly, the role of the private sector and the mass media still remains underexploited. "The spread of education should be an opportunity for industrialisation," said Ms Chung. Besides the manufacturing of technical equipment, school construction and furniture, the expansion of education also produces demand for textbooks: "I have always seen the production of textbooks at the national level as equivalent to the Green Revolution," said Ms Chung. "Just as we reach to have food for all produced locally, so we have to have textbooks for all produced locally." Several countries have taken measures to involve the private sector in the field of basic education. In Brazil, the Ministry of' Education is promoting a series of meetings with sectors not traditionally involved in education, Such as labour and business. In Nigeria, every registered company that employs more, than 500 people, must contribute two per cent of its profits to an Education Fund, managed by a Board of Trustees. The funds for primary education are earmarked for the implementation of the Nine-Year Compulsory Education Programme.

In several of the nine most populous countries, television and radio are starting to play an increasingly active role in disseminating the message of Education for All. The recent expansion of satellite broadcasting provides an opportunity as well as a challenge to policymakers. But to maximise the usefulness and impact of the media, systematic planning is vital. Experience has shown that specific groups must be carefully targeted, be they teachers, bureaucrats, politicians, or the public at large, with well designed materials on the issues that affect them directly. In India, a media strategy developed with the assistance of a professional advertising agency in 1991-1992 led to an intensive media "blitz" of spots and short films through radio, television and government mobile publicity units in support of the Total Literacy Campaigns. An evaluation of the campaign found that the exposure had an important effect in creating greater awareness about the literacy drives, the need for education, and more generally, helped to place literacy higher on the political and social agenda. In Bangladesh, where no more than 2 to 3 per cent of households have television sets, mass media is most valuable in gaining support of the bureaucracy and allied organisations who have access. Nonetheless, there are several initiatives to raise awareness through the media: an animation film, "Meena", was produced with the intent to sensitise people toward gender discrimination in education. In Egypt, the media have been used extensively to inform the public about policies, explain strategies and mobilise family and student support in favour of various initiatives.

Decentralisation

Placing responsibility into the hands of communities entails increased financial autonomy at the local level. Greater success in universalisation of primary education and expansion of basic education opportunities in the nine high-population countries correlates with a higher degree of effective decentralisation in planning, management and control of resources in educational programmes. But although many countries have taken steps to delegate responsibility to local government, the trend toward decentralisation is still in its infancy. In its 1993 Human Development Report, the UNDP calculated the expenditure decentralisation ratio, referring to the percentage of total government expenditure controlled by local government. In Brazil, it turned out to be seven per cent and in Pakistan only 4 per cent. Until the introduction of Compulsory Primary Education in Bangladesh in 1990, government primary schools, that constitute nearly nine-tenths of the system, were largely managed independently from the communities. Although the situation has improved with the setting up of school managing committees and parent-teacher associations, the authority and resources delegated to them are still meagre.

Without resources, real authority and proper training of professionals, local systems of self-government will have little chance of fulfilling their basic functions. Striking a balance between centralisation of general educational policies and the decentralisation of school functionning remains an ongoing challenge in all nine countries.

Shortage of local resources aside, decentralisation can exacerbate regional regional disparities. "Richer communities will provide richer and better-equipped schools," said Ms Chung. "Poorer communities will be locked in lower technology, low skills and low levels of teaching. This is a very serious issue that needs to be addressed. Ways must be found to counteract imbalances." In China, despite a substantial increase in the total budgetary allocations and expenditure on primary education, the real expenditure increase during the last decade has primarily benefitted the urban and better-off rural areas. To reverse this situation, the State Education Commission has been organising the urban areas and economically developed provinces to assist underdeveloped areas in improving primary education.

Additional funds have also been allocated toward the construction of schools and the purchasing of teaching aids in poor areas. In Egypt, the Community Schools Project targets areas in hamlets of poor rural villages. People's participation and management of their own schools is a key element of the proposal. The curriculum content focuses on the development needs of the area and includes health, family life, local history and agriculture. Teaching methods emphasize creativity, problem-solving and learning for service. The Ministry of Education -U N I C E F project, inaugurated in 1992, aims at becoming a non-formal multigrade primary education model with potential for replication and scaling-up.

Despite unanimous consensus on the principle of decentralisation, the floor raised other concerns regarding its practice.

Malini Bhattachavya for instance, warned that decentralisation should not become a pretext for abusive privatisation and profitmaking, phenomena that could lead to increased inequity in access and participation.

A Four-Point Agenda

In reaction to the scale of the Education for All task, Dr Mahbub ul Haq proposed a four-point agenda to participants:

1. Each country must recognise that Education for All is a national priority in which everyone has to be involved. All nonformal means, including the mass media, must be used and more steps taken to delegate responsibility to local government. The experience of NGOs must be tapped, and parents and children involved in choosing their education.
   - The key focus of future efforts must be on education for girls. Removing the existing gender disparities in education will mean that

over the next seven years, for every additional boy, three additional girls will have to be enrolled, said Dr ul Haq. This is not just a question of recruiting more teachers or devoting more resources. It means a transformation of social attitudes. The cost of removing gender disparity is very small. According to one study quoted by Dr. ul Haq, raising the female primary enrolment rate to equal that of boys in low-income countries will cost around $938 million. This is 0. 1 percent of their combined GDP and less than 4 per cent of their defence expenditure. "History could not have offered a better bargain," affirmed Dr ul Haq.

3. Redirecting existing resources will provide the additional $4 billion a year required to achieve EFA. The first and most obvious source in the new political atmosphere following the end of the Cold War is a reduction in military expenditure. If all nine Summit countries agree to freeze their military expenditure and subsequently reduce it by one per cent per year for seven years, this would cumulatively provide about $18 billion which could be directed to meeting basic learning needs. "Let us not forget that the cost of each jet fighter equals one million children in primary school," said Dr. id Haq. "If only the leaders of the nine Summit countries would commit themselves today that in the next seven years; they will buy only 75 fewer jets, the targets of basic education for all would be met. How much more powerful would that one sentence of political commitment be compared to millions of words that flow from such conferences, year in, year out."

   The second main source of funds for primary education is a redirection of Overseas Development

Assistance. At present, the education sector receives about one-tenth of ODA but of this, only about seven per cent is earmarked for primary education. If half of existing educational assistance were earmarked for primary education, this would release an additional $10 billion in aid for primary education over the next seven years.

4. The exchange of experience should be encouraged. Any policy maker should be able to pick up a phone, or access a computer database, to collect all the relevant experience on the problem which she or he is facing. The UNESCO secretariat can act as a valuable facilitator in this regard.

In concluding, Dr ul Haq called for a "grand education compact" based on the above strategies, affirming that the UNDP, under its new flagship of "sustainable human development," was aware that "it, will have to do more - much more-to help meet basic learning needs."

Index